Waller's World

by Roy Waller

Preface by Nigel Worthington

To
PAULINE
LOTS OF LOVE

Preface

When I leave the Norwich City dressing room at the end of each match, about the first person I encounter is Roy Waller. I am always delighted to see him, because, win or lose, Roy is invariably fair in his questions and positive in his comments.

It was a particular joy for me to see him alongside the players and my other colleagues on the balcony of City Hall on the evening of May 10 2004. The thousands of fans saw him as part of Norwich City Football Club. And although he is independent, as every BBC commentator must be, he is part of us. He is the link between our away games and those who cannot travel to them. And he provides a valuable service to those whose health or other circumstances don't allow them to come to Carrow Road.

We at Norwich City are pleased that he has decided to tell the story of Waller's World, and are glad that we form a large part of it.

© Eastern Daily Press

Nigel Worthington
September 2004

Grice Chapman
PUBLISHING

First published in the UK in 2004

Grice Chapman Publishing
The Shire House
Burgh-next-Aylsham
Norwich NR11 6TP

www.gricechapman.com

ISBN 0-9545726-5-3

British Library Cataloguing in Publication Data
A catalogue record of this book is available in the British Library

Illustrations © Karen Fuller
www.beauxartsbindings.co.uk

Designed and printed by Barnwell's Print Ltd
Aylsham, Norfolk, NR11 6ET, UK
Tel: +44 (0) 1263 732767

www.barnwellprint.co.uk

Acknowledgements

I decided to write Waller's World because I think there are many people around like me, who do not do so well at school, drift into a job or two, and then have a mundane working life which gives them little satisfaction. That was me until not that long ago when I decided to do something about it. And the lesson is that if you don't enjoy your work, you must act to help yourself.

The kind of life I lead and enjoy now would not have been possible without my day-to-day involvement in two great British institutions – the BBC and Norwich City Football Club. So I would like to thank the present and past managers of BBC Radio Norfolk for giving me the opportunity to practise my craft, and for successfully persuading me to take up broadcasting full-time after I had spent nearly a quarter of a century with the Automobile Association. I would also like to thank my colleagues at the BBC for all their help and advice and in particular David Clayton who made it all possible. I must also thank the directors, players, and supporters of Norwich City for the help and encouragement they have always given me.

I am grateful to Colin Chapman, chairman of Grice Chapman Publishing, himself a former BBC correspondent, for suggesting I write this book, and for helping me with it. Susan Grice has proved an efficient editor. Simon Chapman and Paul Dickson have also been very helpful. I would also like to thank Archant for allowing us to republish some of the photographs that appeared in the *Eastern Daily Press* and *Eastern Evening News* at the time of Norwich's promotion.

Finally I would like to thank my wife Sylvie for her continued support, guidance and loyalty. She was there for me in the good and sometimes the bad times and her advice has kept me on the straight and narrow.

Sylvie's contribution to my afternoon radio programme has been immense and I would like to publicly thank her for love and understanding. I am a very difficult man to live with mainly because I am a Virgo which must drive her mad at times, but I love her to bits and would not change her for the world.

Contents

Neil Adams on Roy Waller

Roy Waller, Radio Norfolk legend, is generally a nice guy.

Right, that's enough of the niceties, because unlike myself, who, of course, am faultless to a tee, there are plenty of facts with which I can embarrass my old mate.

When he told me he was writing this book I was not the least bit surprised – for, after all, enough people know him, and he should have a tale or two to tell from his 80-odd years on this planet. But he was pulled up short when I deflated his ego in an instant by asking him for an early copy so I could stop my kitchen table from wobbling. One of its legs is shorter than the other, and I cannot think of a better use for a book by Roy Waller.

The first thing that anyone who has had the pleasure of knowing Roy learns is that 'punctuality' should be his middle name.

He is always on time, absolutely guaranteed to be. The problem is that the poor sods who have to travel with him to wherever Norwich City are playing, namely yours truly, every other Saturday in the football season, soon realise that this is because he gets to his destination hours before he needs to.

"Can't be late for a live radio broadcast, can we?" he asks, rhetorically. "We're not like the journos." How many times have I heard that over the past three seasons?

Arriving at away games long before they have even opened the ground is nothing new any more. Our personal best was when we sat in a deserted car park in Coventry eating our packed lunches at precisely 10.40 am for a 3.00 pm kick-off. Four hours and twenty minutes early – not bad, eh?

Then there is his love of country and western music. That drives me mad, it does. They should pipe his Saturday morning 'rodeo' show through the speakers of every prison in the country. That would reduce the crime rate – I guarantee you.

He has also been known to get the occasional name wrong in his commentaries. Live radio commentary is not an easy task, by any means, and Roy is very good at it, but he can't be spared the times he has, for some strange reason, mixed up a few letters of the players' names. For example, Gerry Taggart became Terry Gaggart, and Vinny Samways became Sammy Vinways. It was not so funny when he messed up with Crewe Alexandra's midfield player, Kenny Lunt.

Like most 80-year-olds Waller cannot take his drink. I had already heard about his drunken stupor in the San Siro before the Norwich game against Inter Milan ten years back, when some irresponsible BBC colleagues virtually forced him to down the copious amount of two glasses of red wine. Then I witnessed it for myself at the end of last season during a meal in a Thai restaurant.

On this occasion Roy must have drunk at least two shandies and an Irish coffee before staggering up to the bar and asking, of all things, for the Yellow Pages – because he could not remember where he lived, and wanted to go home.

Finally, I suppose I should mention the great delight he takes in deriding the young, healthy super-fit summarizer who turns up at each away game with a nice cosy travel blanket to keep his legs warm during the matches. Funny how "You big soppy tart" can turn into a "Let me have a bit of your blanket, please" by a quarter past four!

So, Good Luck Roy. I have absolutely no doubts whatsoever that he will make enough money from the proceeds of his book to pay back the five quid he owes me!

Neil Adams
September 2004

Chapter 1
A Dream Come True

I set my alarm clock for ten to three in the morning, not my favourite waking hour. When its shrillness pierced the darkened room I awoke, full of apprehension. Why, oh why, had I taken on that bet in the rashness of the Christmas holiday season, foolishly promising that if Darren Huckerby signed for the Canaries, I would run naked through the streets of Norwich?

It had seemed a safe, if attention grabbing, gamble at Christmas. Darren had completed a fruitful three-month loan period at Carrow Road, where the fans had taken him to their hearts, but he had gone back to his Premiership club, Manchester City. Nigel Worthington had played down the prospect of Norwich City signing either Huckerby or his other loan player, Peter Crouch, while Neil Doncaster, the club's chief executive, made it abundantly clear that both Darren's wage expectations and Manchester City's transfer fee were unaffordable.

In any case a large number of well-endowed clubs were after Huckerby, including City's rivals West Bromwich Albion, where manager Gary Megson was not slow to let the press know that he was in talks to lure Worthington's most wanted man to The Hawthorns.

Up in Manchester manager Kevin Keegan was also insisting he would only part company with Huckerby for a very high price. And to cap it all, Huckerby's agent had abrasively told the *Eastern Daily Press* that his client would "definitely not be going to Norwich".

As I crept downstairs taking care not to wake my wife, Sylvie, I ruefully reflected on how I had ignored key signals that had pointed otherwise; for instance his insistence after what many, including me, thought was his "farewell" appearance against Cardiff City, when he said: "Get it sorted, and I'll be back." Significantly there were also frequent visits by Huckerby to Norwich estate agents specialising in up-market property, and dinners he and his wife enjoyed together at their comfortable hotel at the end of his loan period. Of course the main signal came after my foolhardy promise, when Darren went on record to say: "If I do not sign for Norwich I sign for no one."

I drove the short journey from Eaton to the City Centre hoping I could fulfil my promise without attracting attention. Norwich is not perhaps the best lit of cities in Britain but as I reached St Stephens it seemed ablaze with light.

How could I fulfil my promise without being noticed? It would be highly embarrassing if I was spotted, recognised or, worse, photographed. At least there were no policemen lurking in the doorways as in the old days when at night there would be an officer on the beat.

I parked the car in the square, looked around to make sure there was no one about, and quickly stripped off. Now for it, I thought. The night air was cool and dank. I was out of the car like a startled rabbit, and streaked round Gentlemen's Walk, up the hill to City Hall and back again, taking care not to be within sight of the main police station opposite the Forum and the BBC studios. I went very quickly round that square I can tell you – the pigeons were amazed. Out of breath, I panted back to the car, jumped in, donned my light clothes, and was off, back home to a warm bed. Nobody had seen me, there were no photographs. I had done it!

Iwan Roberts: gap tooth giant strikes again
© Eastern Daily Press

One evening, just a few days later on May 10, I was back in the Market Place, but this time on the balcony of City Hall with the Norwich City squad and the directors and management. Where the lone streaker had ventured a few nights earlier, there was now a sea of yellow and green. Down below and across as far as the eye could see there were fans cheering, holding placards and waving giant banners. The police told us there were 50,000 people there, which is more than twice the number that crams into the newly enlarged Carrow Road for the best-attended games.

I had never before seen anything like it. Although there had been a similar if smaller celebration in the same place in May 2002 when Norwich returned from the Millennium Stadium after being beaten to the Premiership by Birmingham City, this time there was no sadness, only wild, exuberant happiness, for Norwich City had earned the right to play in the world's best football league.

The 50,000 people had come out to see their heroes. They seemed to have filled every crack and crevice within sight. They were on rooftops and leaning out of windows, even atop of lampposts. There were children perched on their fathers' shoulders, and old people leaning on sticks. Those who were in the best positions to see the players had been there all day. As the time came for the Division One trophy to be presented to captain Adam Drury the excitement mounted and the noise was deafening. There were horns, whistles and an assortment of musical instruments, as well as singing, chanting and cheering. Adam lifted the huge trophy with its trailing ribbons high above his head, and thousands of cameras flashed and clicked as the crowd became delirious with joy. Then each player, and Nigel Worthington and Delia Smith, took turns to lift the trophy, prompting more roars from the fans. There seemed to be electricity in the

Darren Huckerby, Norwich's soccer pontiff, surveys his flock © Eastern Daily Press

air. Ticker tape was released from the roof of City Hall, and fluttered down past us towards the mass of yellow and green. On the roof a huge replica Canary grinned as it presided over the joyous proceedings. The players danced with joy as a formation of nine Jaguars from RAF Coltishall screamed overhead in a hi-tech salute to East Anglia's proudest football team.

Some of the players had brought their families. Malky Mackay, whose headed goals and commanding defensive performance, had earned the Canaries essential points came out with his wife Pamela and baby Callum, whom he had clutched so proudly in the lap of honour after the final victorious home game against Preston. There was City hero of many years, Iwan Roberts, doing his best to hide his disappointment at not being given a chance to play in the Premiership. His replacement, Leon McKenzie, wore a broad grin and spoke for the entire squad when he said it was a dream come true.

I glanced to my right and there was Darren Huckerby, peering almost nonchalantly towards the crowd. As he soaked up the warmth of the fans hero worshipping him he seemed quite subdued. I moved across to him, shook him by the hand, and asked him how he felt. He replied, simply: "It's worked out quite well."

Nigel Worthington was very emotional. On two or three occasions he was reduced to tears. You would not expect that kind of thing from Nigel, because he is a man who is very much on an even keel. But on the balcony and later on the top of the bus touring the city he was overcome. He accepted and appreciated what the fans had done. They had supported him and the team through thick and thin, and now they were sharing the triumph. Nigel knows above all how important the supporters are, and he appreciated that when, during the season, he called for their support and asked them to be more vocal, they responded magnificently.

'It's my turn': Roy shows off the Division One trophy with Nigel Worthington

Nigel was asked when he first believed the team would win the title, and replied: "Neil Warnock (Sheffield United), Joe Royle (Ipswich Town), Alan Pardew (West Ham) and one or two others started saying we could not do it. I decided in my mind we could do it. We have done it."

Below, the crowd were singing with gusto: "We are the champions." There were the usual jibes at the tractor boys, against whom we had enjoyed two convincing wins, and put Joe Royle in his place. To do the double over Ipswich Town, the old enemy, was in itself cause for celebration.

And then someone must have spotted me, for the next song was "There's only one Roy Waller, there's only one Roy Waaallerr." Transfixed, I felt a lump in my throat. I had a sudden intake of breath, and my eyes watered. I began to gulp, and I had to turn and walk back inside to recover my composure.

To be recognised and get that kind of acclaim was the highlight of my career. I knew the fans had not come there to see me, but I was part of it. As if to confirm it Nigel came over and insisted I had my photograph taken with the team and their coveted trophy.

There was more of the same as I was invited to join the team on their top-of-bus tour round the city. It was non-stop pandemonium: more songs, more cheers, more tears, and unstoppable unbridled celebration. As the evening shadows fell on this sunny spring evening we were driven around the dear, familiar streets of my home city for more than an hour, but it seemed only minutes, before it was all over.

As I walked back to my car parked near the Forum, more fans came up and shook my hand, or put their arms round me. "Well done for the commentary with you and Neil," they said. "You kept us informed."

I drove back home to Eaton reflecting that no broadcaster could ask for a better tribute. And I thought back on my days as a child growing up in Norwich and playing with my tape recorder when a job at the BBC had seemed beyond my wildest dreams. To be the BBC Radio Norfolk reporter covering Norwich City as they marched into the Premiership was indeed a dream come true.

Robert Green: 'ready for England'

Chapter 2
The Education of Young Roy

I was born on September 17 1940 and raised in Norfolk. The county has always been my home, and always will be. I like to travel, both in England and overseas, but I have no desire to live anywhere else. For me Norwich is the focal point of Waller's World.

I was brought up in the Mile Cross area to the north of the city, just inside the outer ring road. It was very much an area in which you had to survive, a kind of neighbourhood with attitude. I am very proud of my roots; they provided me with lots of adventures. In those days we had no fear.

I was a war baby. Hitler's Luftwaffe had its sights on Norfolk's many Royal Air Force fields, and Norwich, as the most easterly of Britain's industrial cities, was also a prime target. My father was away serving in the Army, so we lived with my grandmother and grandfather at 20 Rye Close. I saw very little of my father at the time. I remember as a small child being amazed suddenly to see a man in full uniform appear in the doorway. At the time I could not understand who this man was, but it was indeed my father, bless him.

Everything was rationed. Ration books were issued by the Ministry of Food. Many of the everyday items we simply take for granted now were scarce, very expensive or not available at all. We children did not see a banana, orange or even an ice cream until after the war.

At the age of five I was sent to the Norman School. It is the only school I have ever attended, starting with the infants, then the juniors, and then moving up. I wasn't much good at school, except at sport, which I loved. I preferred the holidays when I would spend a lot of time with my Dad, who by then had returned to his job with the Swan Laundry. I would go out with him in his van, and we would pick up stuff from a number of places. One of them was Caleys, the chocolate manufacturer, and I really looked forward to going there because they would give us a big bag of Caleys' waste, all deliciously stuck together. What a treat! The other thing that was enormous fun was to ride down the shoot at the Swan Laundry where the laundry came out. They were lovely days.

In the holidays I'd spend most of the days outside, going out at eight in the morning and coming back at six in the evening. In the summer I'd swim in the

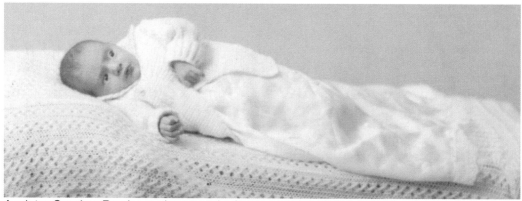
A winter Sunday: Roy learns how to take it easy

Wensum river: that was where I learned to swim. But it was also to lead to the first big setback in my life. I contracted diphtheria.

Diphtheria was the disease every parent dreaded. At the time there were posters in public places warning of its consequences, frequently fatal. I remember my young body seizing up: I could not walk, I could not even move. The doctor was called and they took me off from Rye Close in an ambulance. My father, who was at work at the time, arrived home to see the vehicle pulling away down the street, and jumped back into his car to follow me to the hospital.

I was placed in an isolation unit at the West Norwich Hospital. I can remember it to this day. It was like an open garage, I was in the garage part and there were no doors. It was exposed to the elements, the wind and the rain came in, and then, later, driven snow. There was plenty of fresh air, for that was the idea.

I was paralysed from the waist down, and the prognosis for getting better, let alone playing football again, was not good. But the treatments slowly worked. I was fed a diet of fish. I can't stand it now: you won't find me queuing up at the counter of the local fish and chip shop at the end of match days.

Even illness has its up sides. In the next ward, or 'garage', to mine, there was a very nice older guy who kept a friendly eye on me, and offered words of encouragement. Better still, he played the harmonica. Every night I would hear the strains of Don't Fence Me In, a highly appropriate tune for our location and illness. It was a song that I took to my heart, and now that I have a harmonica of my own I play it often and relive the moment. I tried to track him down recently because I wanted to thank him for lifting my spirits all those years ago. Unfortunately I was unsuccessful, for at the time he lived in the centre of Norwich and many of the homes that were once there have been pulled down for redevelopment. I would love to hear from him again.

A highlight, as I got better, was to go to the cinema. I had this long wicker chair on wheels, and they would push me into the darkened theatre through special doors, and park me in the aisle. This kind of thing was quite special in those days; it was long before authorities started making special provision for disabled people.

It took a long while to recover. Eventually I regained my strength, and the paralysis receded. Back at school I gradually got back to playing sport, and later on had a trial for Norwich Boys. Whether debilitated by having had diphtheria I don't know, but I was a pretty sickly child. I was a boy who caught everything; all the main children's diseases, measles, mumps, chicken pox and so on. I had my adenoids out, and my tonsils were removed.

There were three occasions when my mother saved my life because her remarkable intuition told her things were not right for me. One of these occasions was when I had suspected meningitis. Noticing a discharge from my ears she managed to turn me over so it ran out and did not enter my brain. I owe her a lot, and my grandma too. One of my early memories is being taken out in a pushchair to find a place where they were repairing the roads. Once there she would push me along behind the tar lorry in the belief that the fumes from the tar would stop me from becoming ill again. Did it work? Well, I am still here to tell the tale.

The other highlight of my life, of course, was going to see Norwich City. My father was a regular supporter of the Canaries, but at six years old I was judged to be too young to be taken to see the first team. Those were the days when you had to stand on the terraces. So he would take me to see the reserves. But then when I got a bit older came the day when he relented to my pressure and said: "Yes, you can attend the first team."

It was an exciting day, but I cannot remember whom Norwich was playing. I do remember being taken to the South Stand where my father, my uncle and a friend would occupy the exact same spot each week, surrounded always by the same people. As a small boy you could not see much, but the people around welcomed the new supporter, and always made room for me. Invariably at five to three a giant of a man would come and stand bang in front of me. Then I would have to wriggle around and make sure I could see something.

We had a lovely time one Easter Monday when, in line with tradition, there would be a match between King's Lynn and Great Yarmouth during the morning, which we would watch, and then in the afternoon Norwich played. In between games my father took me to the pub in King Street just across Carrow Bridge. He and his companions would be in there having a pint, and I would be outside with a bottle of fizzy lemonade and a packet of crisps, before heading back into the ground for the real excitement.

So that was my early introduction to Norwich City Football Club and to the

The street where Roy grew up: Rye Close in Mile Cross

With Mother and Father

Canaries. From then on I grew up with them. I loved every minute. After walking to the ground and clanking our way through the turnstiles, we then witnessed the magical way the atmosphere of the crowd built up. We stood on old railway sleepers, which would not pass today's health and safety regulations. Suddenly there would be a roar as the players came out of the tunnel. There was a wonderful atmosphere around us with people shouting, and getting involved with the game, and of course I was carried along with it. There were long faces if Norwich lost and joy if they won. Football was right at the heart of the city community then, partly because there were fewer alternatives. People did not play golf, or go off to leisure centres, which did not exist. We all went to the football on a Saturday, everyone from the Bishop of Norwich to the boys from Mile Cross. That was the thing to do.

After the game there were the football results on radio and the *Pink Un* pushed through the door by home delivery. We would read that on a Saturday night and relive the game we had just seen, or, if the Canaries were away, read a blow-by-blow account of the 90 minutes. There was inevitably much more about the game, and less about the footballers' personalities and private lives. Remember that footballers in those days, although they were heroes, led a much more simple life than today. Some had part time jobs, selling cars or whatever, and they did not earn a great deal of money. If Norwich were away you did not have live commentaries coming to you, and so when the football results came through on a Saturday evening it was mandatory that everyone in the house had to be quiet. Father needed to check his football coupons, to see if the time spent before the fire in an armchair on a midweek evening would yield any profit. It seldom did.

Compared with the fun of Saturdays, school was a bit of an anti-climax. I was not good in class, and was absolutely terrible at maths. I was not too bad in English. But I failed the 11-plus, and did not get any A-levels. I did enjoy amateur dramatics, and was very good at sport, having overcome the handicap caused by diphtheria. I adored football, cricket, and tennis, whatever. Mostly through sport I made quite a number of good friends at school, and am still in

Roy at school: 'not good in class'

The Norman at Mile Cross: Roy's one and only school

touch with some of them. I was a good bowler, and would play cricket with boys who were three or four years older than me, and hold my own. I was not much of a batsman, but my bowling skills kept me in the team.

Outside school we had a few dust ups. There were running battles with the boys from the Woodcock Road area. There were boundaries between our area and theirs, and if you crossed them there would be trouble. It was very territorial. In school my activities led one teacher to say to me, gravely: "Waller, you will finish up in prison." It was amusing to meet him more than three decades later after I had joined the BBC, when he greeted me by saying: "Waller, you have done well for yourself."

Some of my classmates did end up in prison, partly because they came from an area where there was no money. I remember we were all issued with school plimsolls with their sizes stamped on them; some of the boys were so poor they had no other footwear and so they wore the school issue outside at evenings and weekends. The same was true of school shorts.

Eventually the time came when I had to decide on a career. I had this wonderful theory that I was going to be a journalist, not realising of course that I had no qualifications whatsoever. This was quickly pointed out to me.

As a teenage hobby on dark evenings I would script, produce and record audio drama. I would therefore record imaginary radio commentaries. Someone had given me one of those old reel-to-reel tape recorders, and I would pretend to be a broadcaster reporting on live events, creating my own sound effects as background.

I would play them back to the family, who were bored stiff with them. They were driven mad as there was a "Vroom, Vroom, this is Roy Waller at Brands Hatch, we're just on the starting grid…. Vroom, Vroom, and they're off." For tennis I would hold my index finger in my mouth and make a popping sound like a tennis ball dropping on to court, and then imitate the Wimbledon umpire with a rather upper-crust "30-40...Deuce...Game to Hoad and Rosewall" (two Australian tennis heroes of the time). Today's listeners would find my teenage football commentaries more familiar: "It's an open goal, he must score, oh he's missed it, how could he miss that!"

Enjoyable as this hobby was for me, if not my family, it was fantasy to believe I could get a job in broadcasting. Other people did but Waller had to be realistic, and earn his living in a more modest manner.

Chapter 3
Taking the Mike

I realised I could not be a journalist; that was a silly idea. So my first job was with the Norwich estate agent, Hanbury Williams. I forget what I was called at the time, but in truth I was the office boy. I made the tea and did the filing. Slightly more interesting was getting out of the office and attending auctions, where I had to make a note of the names of bidders and what they had bought. I would also go out and put up posters of pending sales, and set up 'sold' boards when a property had changed hands.

It did not take me long to realise that this was not the life for me. So then, like many thousands of Norfolk people over the years, I joined the Norwich Union, where I was placed in the fire insurance underwriting department. It was not much better than the estate agency, but as the young rascal I was at the time, I learned a trick or two that worked in a large organization such as the Norwich Union.

I discovered that if you walked around confidently with a piece of paper in your hand nobody would ever come up to you and say, "What are you doing?" It was an excellent way of relieving the tedium of a mundane office life. So, for instance, I would go out of the Surrey Street office and enjoy a hot drink round the corner at the coffee bar. Or I would pick up a piece of paper and wander off into four or five different departments and sometimes chat to people there. Sometimes I would stroll across to Bonds, now John Lewis, and attend a fashion show. The Norwich Union was such a large place that nobody really knew or cared what you did.

If it lacked excitement or interest it was also very undemanding. But then one Saturday morning - office workers worked Saturday mornings in those days - one of my many superiors rebuked me for coming to work in a purple shirt. What, I asked myself, was wrong with a purple shirt on what was traditionally a dress-down, sports jacket day? I realised then that the Norwich Union was not the place for me.

My third job was to last longer. I saw an advertisement in the *Eastern Evening News* that said the Automobile Association wanted staff at its regional headquarters in Thorpe Road. So I applied, I went for an interview, and then a second, and then they offered me a choice of jobs – I could be a receptionist, work in overseas touring, or in membership. I plumped for the overseas touring job: I thought that would be interesting. I was second in command handling car bookings to the Continent.

I was to spend 24 years and nine months at the AA, working in a variety of areas, ending up as co-ordinator in the breakdown department. For many years I worked 12-hour shifts. The night shift from eight in the evening until eight in the morning was often frustrating, because for much of the time you ended up with nothing to do. Looking back on it now it was a waste of my life: I could and should have been doing something more interesting. But the AA also provided what previously had been unthinkable – a gateway to a broadcasting career.

At that time there was no such thing as local radio. All we had were small segments of news, travel and sport that were dropped into the national programmes transmitted by the BBC from its mast in Tacolneston just to the south of Norwich.

The AA would provide the one-minute travel reports from East Anglia, and I took on the job of doing them. The segment was called *Round About East Anglia* and I went to the BBC's Norwich television studios to record them. One of the producers there, Mike Chapman, told me he thought I was a good broadcaster, and suggested I take it up as a career. I said "no" because there were no jobs in Norfolk, and I quite enjoyed working at the AA with some lovely people.

But then came the day when I was asked to go down to AA headquarters at Fanum House in Teddington, where I saw the top man there. He told me it seemed to him I was wasting my career there. "Why don't you leave and try the Norwich Union?" he asked. Been there, done that. So he said, "Well try the UEA"(the University of East Anglia). This meeting made me uneasy. I kept

thinking, "Why is he telling me this?"

Back in Norwich my mind churned over my future. I had a comfortable and supposedly secure job and I was earning a good living. But life was passing me by, and I just felt in my heart of hearts that I was not doing the right thing. At the AA I had played at being a broadcaster, just as I had as a teenager. I had put together radio sketches for the office Christmas parties, acting as the linkman. I had been issued with one of those large dictation machines into which I would dictate letters, and I came up with the idea of taking it out into the street to interview passers-by on what they thought of the AA. It seemed a good idea at the time, and the people being interviewed thought it was for real, that they were being recorded.

My bosses, however, were not overly impressed with this attempt at market research. They thought I was just playing the fool. At this particular time I was not getting on too well with my boss, who, whenever anything went wrong, assumed it had to be my fault. I always will remember him saying to me: "You are no good to anyone here; you are always messing around."

There was another chance development, which turned out to be an essential conduit to my broadcasting career. I was in the habit of spending some of my spare time with the Association for the Blind in Norwich. I had a couple of relatives who were blind. And so I often used to go down to their club to keep them company and have a chat. One Saturday afternoon all the men were sitting around smoking – and listening to a football commentary that was coming through a loudspeaker. "Oh, that's the football from Carrow Road: it is the Hospital Sports Commentary Service", I was told. I thought it was brilliant. They told me that the service even covered Norwich's away matches, by using the opposing team's city's hospital sports facilities. A lovely man there called

Dickie Gosling spent some time telling me all about it, and then, to my delight, said, "Are you interested in doing this?" I said I would love to. But I did not think any more of it until a few weeks later when I got a call at the AA. "I understand you are interested in joining the Hospitals Sports Commentary Service," said the caller. I said I was. "Then come down to Carrow Road this Saturday, make yourself known at the commentary box and we will give you five minutes."

The next weekend I found the box right at the back of the old South Stand, above and behind where I used to go with Father. I knocked on the door, and introduced myself to Cyril Robinson, the man in charge. At the wide desk in front of me sat four commentators, all with headphones and microphones. "We will give you five minutes in a moment," Cyril said. Soon one of them came off the seat at the front, and I jumped in. I finished up recording 20 minutes. Sitting on my immediate left was a director of Colmans. At the end he turned to me and said: "You're good." But he continued – and this has stuck in my mind whenever I do live soccer commentaries – "Please let the listener know where the ball is. That's important."

There and then I was invited to join one of their regular teams. John Taylor was in charge of my team, and we would do 20 minutes each. From time to time people went sick, and so I filled in for them. I would also report reserve games. They were very different from first team performances, because you would be the only commentator. Being on the South Stand side, we were opposite where the players came out of the tunnel, too far away to be able to pick up the team news.

I remember with not a little embarrassment one game when I had a guy scoring three goals and he was not even on the pitch! Covering these games was tremendous ground work for my later BBC commentating career, for it involved talking for a full 90 minutes on my own, watching players I did not really know. This was especially true of the away team, and there were no programme notes to help.

Even so I thoroughly enjoyed it. It was just me, talking non-stop, ready to add colour whenever the play demanded. I developed my own style of painting word pictures, describing exactly what I could see; a bird flying into the top of the stand, or someone wearing a bright coloured hat, or a cloud with perhaps an aeroplane cutting through it.

Life was fun, and my weekends were increasingly busy. And then one winter's day I picked up my copy of the *Eastern Evening News*, and read that the BBC was bringing local radio to Norwich. Those interested were invited to come to the Maids Head Hotel in Norwich to learn more. My transition to full-time broadcaster was about to begin.

Chapter 4
BBC World

There was snow on the ground on the Friday night when I trudged down Tombland to the Maids Head Hotel; it was the kind of evening when most Norwich people would be at home in front of the television. I was unprepared for what I found, for the hotel ballroom was absolutely packed with people.

I queued up and eventually got to the front where a rather hurried BBC regional news editor, Ian Hyams, greeted me.

"What can I do for you?" he asked with the wearied look of a man who has had enough and was looking forward to his evening meal.

I took the plunge. "Well it's more a question of what I can do for you," I said, firmly.

Ian brightened. "I have not heard that all night," he said. "What do you want to do?"

I told him what I did, and said I would like to do live football commentaries for the fledgling BBC Radio Norfolk. He said: "Give me your name and address," and that was that. I went back home through the snow, not wholly confident I would ever hear from him again.

Two weeks went by. Then the phone rang and the BBC asked me to go down to Carrow Road the following Saturday where they would record a mock programme.

When I got to the football ground I was provided with a microphone and headphones, and when I put these on I found I was connected to the BBC studios in the city. On the other end of the line was someone called Mike Souter. Assisted at my end by a producer, I was briefed to describe the game and periodically answer questions posed by Mike. I remember they were very hard questions, but I fielded them to the best of my ability. At the end of the game they thanked me in a non-committal way, and said they would be in touch.

Again I waited – I learned to expect that of the BBC, where there is a lot of waiting – but then the call came and I was invited in to see the station manager, Mike Cheney, who engaged me to cover Norwich City's home games. It was not the practice then to cover away matches: the BBC took a telephone feed from either the local BBC station or an agency.

So there I was: I had become a football commentator for the BBC. I kept my job at the AA. By working

'Oh Referee! You can't be serious'

great Norfolk character. He had been covering the Canaries for some time, he'd seen it all and he knew it all. One of his famous memories was being thrown off the team bus by one of City's more tenacious managers, Ron Saunders. We formed a good team. In those days I had the additional task, after the game, of having to run down the gantry stairs and rush back to the studio to air a quick report. Quite often the studio announcer would be saying something like: "Norwich City 3, Portsmouth 0, Roy Waller was at Carrow Road" as, breathless, I sat down at the microphone.

There were no interviews in those days, because technically there was no way we could do them.

Soon it was decided that our reports of home games were so popular that I should also cover the away fixtures. Until then we had depended on local BBC stations for coverage, but this did not always work if there were several clubs within a station's area.

through lunch and acquiring compensatory hours I was able to organize myself to cover the home games once a fortnight

In those days the radio commentator was positioned high up on the television gantry in the South Stand, well away from the main stand where the dugouts and the tunnel are, and where the manager operated. In the harsh winters it was freezing cold and, to make matters worse, we had the PA system's speakers close by our commentary point. When it was in use it was impossible to know whether the listeners could hear the recording.

The BBC provided me with what is called a summarizer, who chips in from time to time with a comment or observation, allowing the commentator to draw his breath and take a swig from a bottle of water. That was how I met Keith Skipper, who at the time was a producer with Radio Norfolk. Skip, as everyone calls him, was and remains a

'Why do they keep giving the ball away?'

In the commentary box: Roy, Neil and the rug

My immediate problem was that I would not have a summarizer and would have to report the 90 minutes all by myself. Keith did not want to travel: he hates leaving the county and for him to venture beyond Thetford is like going abroad.

The first away match was a bit of an adventure. I was given directions from the local station which were simply "Head for the floodlights," I ended up driving round a railway marshalling yard.

Driving by myself was a bit tedious on very long journeys, so I started using the supporters' coaches; the BBC liked that because it was cheap. All went well until one evening after recording a final wrap-up I came out of Anfield to get the bus home only to watch it disappear out of the car park. The local police had decided they wanted to get the Norwich supporters away without delay. How, I wondered, would I get back to Norfolk? I was sure there would not be a train, and anyway cross-country trains at weekends are notoriously unreliable. Fortunately I spotted the football reporter from the *Eastern Daily Press*, and he was kind enough to give me a lift in his car.

Now, of course, I have Neil Adams for company. On the long drives together he grumbles a bit, but he's a good companion, and knows where the best eating places are.

Chapter 5
No Gold Watch or Cuckoo Clock

I was still working for the Automobile Association but becoming increasingly restless. The work was sometimes tiresome, but what bothered me were the repeated rumours that my job was not quite as secure as I had thought.

I was also really happy doing my radio work. I looked forward to Saturdays at Carrow Road. I was becoming known as "Roy Waller, who does the football commentaries", and for the first time in my life I felt proud to be recognised for something I did.

I believe in fate; some things in your life that are mapped out for you. A colleague from the AA came down from the Midlands and said: "Hey, you want to move on because the AA in Norwich is going to be streamlined, and jobs are going to be moved to the Midlands. Unless you are prepared to move, you are going to find yourself without a job."

There was no way I was going to move to Birmingham or Coventry or somewhere like that. So I decided to do what my mother had advised so many years earlier: improve my skills and knowledge. Radio was my game, but I had to make it more than a game on a Saturday. I had to find out how programmes were run, how decisions were made, and how a radio station like Radio Norfolk really worked. And I had to do it fast.

So whenever I had time to spare, particularly in the evenings, I would go up to Norfolk Towers, that hideous building where the BBC had their production suites, and start learning. I decided to follow the sports editor, Rob Bonnett, now on national television, and find out what he did. I would answer the phones and generally make myself useful, but my real goal was to see how programmes were produced. It was a wonderful learning curve; I learnt so much from that man. I am sure they found it useful to have me around. Everyone knew me from my football commentaries, and I think they were pleased I took an interest in what went on behind the scenes.

My learning plan worked even better than I could have wished. After a few weeks I was asked if I would like to present a soccer special programme one evening. At first I was rather daunted by the challenge, but I never considered declining the offer. I am a great believer in saying "yes", and then worrying about it later. When you actually do it, the fear of failure usually disappears, and you wonder why you were so worried in the first place.

Norfolk Towers: grim former home of Radio Norfolk

The presenter of the afternoon show became pregnant, and the BBC asked me if I would like to join the Corporation full-time. I surprised myself by not leaping at the chance. It was, in fact, a very tricky decision, and I knew it would take me a long time to make up my mind.

I had been with the AA for 24 years, and I had a pension and job security. Even if they decided to run down the Norwich operation I would still qualify for a redundancy payment if I chose not to move away from Norwich. The BBC offer, though full-time, was a one-year contract not a staff job. There was no pension: you had to fund your own. It was precarious. If I made a mess of it or they did not like me, I would be out of work. On the other hand, if I stayed at the AA I could still do my Saturday football commentaries for Radio Norfolk and other part-time work that came along. I mulled it over. I agonised; the pendulum swung this way and that.

I could sense the BBC's impatience. Here was Waller – who had pushed for work, made efforts to learn the trade, and had made himself available whenever he spotted an opportunity – procrastinating. There were others who would have liked to take over the afternoon programme, and the BBC wanted to tie up a contract.

So I did it, despite all my reservations. The moment I gave in my notice at the AA, I knew it was the right thing to do. The AA human resources manager said rather sniffily, "Well, if you had waited to complete 25 years' service you could have had a long service gift, a cuckoo clock or something." "Oh really?" I said. Because I was short of the 25 years' employment, they gave me a paperweight as my leaving present. I was forced to return my AA membership card, not even allowing me to run it out until the end of the year. Can you believe that? I had devoted a quarter century to the AA. I went straight out and joined their rival, the

And so I took on the soccer special. I have to say I did not make a great start, because I began by playing the wrong record *Mississippi* by Pussy Cat. I remember it to this day. I talked my way out of it, and then I thought: "That wasn't too bad." I am not sure that many people noticed.

I was then offered the chance to sit in for Keith Skipper, who presented the lunchtime programme on Radio Norfolk, and that went well enough. I could not be Keith Skipper, of course. It is a big mistake to try and be like someone else. It never works. You have to be yourself, and develop your own style. So that is what I did.

Stand-ins for several other presenters followed during holiday periods and when they were ill. The AA was becoming less and less appealing compared with my moonlighting for the BBC.

Then the big opportunity arrived.

Moment of joy: Delia and Nigel lift the cup

Former England captain Alan Shearer talks to Roy

'Over to you Roy, sum up the game in 25 seconds'

Wedded bliss: Roy and Sylvie celebrate their wedding at a church blessing

'I'm a country boy, really'

'Can they take much more of this?' wonders Daniel O'Donnell

Roy with the late Adam Faith

It's always good to tee–off after a morning in the studio

'The Norwich Union can't complain about my dress code this time'

Well branded hot hatch

The Forum: smart new home of BBC Radio Norfolk

Roy in charge at SAS ground control

The boss: The BBC's David Clayton with Roy

Dolores and the SAS

There had not been much wrong with the previous afternoon programme, but I knew I had to come up with something different. Afternoon is a tricky time for local radio. In most places the largest audiences are to be found in what we call drive time. In the mornings people are getting up, getting ready for the day ahead, perhaps preparing children for school, and often jumping into a car, where they switch on the radio. The same happens in reverse in the early evenings. At drive time you can often find the whole family listening to the radio. During the day the audience pattern is different. There are still people out and about in their cars, of course, and then there are those remaining at home, be they retired people, shift workers, or those caring for a young family.

In mid-afternoon there is a great deal of choice in broadcasting, ranging from television soaps and repeats to pop music and radio plays. What, I asked myself, could I provide that would have appeal in Norfolk? I also had to bear in mind management's brief – they wanted to get local women not just listening in but also participating.

As I pondered this, I tried to imagine the listener at home, or in a car. In the case of the latter, he or she might be on a boring drive, or stuck in traffic. A person at home might be doing the ironing, or dusting or sitting down to some routine chores, perhaps looking out of the window at grey skies and a world beyond.

Windows! That is what I would do. I would create windows of imagination that people could use to home in on a different world. Radio is made for the imagination. Each story, each word in a sound broadcast, conveys a different picture to each listener, as they visualise in their minds what they are hearing. I decided that I would try and create a World of Waller, taking

RAC, and have not had anything to do with the AA ever since.

I felt a warm glow when I entered Norfolk Towers for my first day as a full-time employee of the British Broadcasting Corporation. I was greeted by David Clayton, the managing editor, who said, with an air of some ceremony: "Roy Waller, I am going to make you a superstar." I was taken aback. I suppose I should have said: "Yes." In the AA or Norwich Union I might have said: "Thank you, sir." It did not seem real. So I replied, trying very hard not to sound ungrateful: "No you are not. You are just giving me the opportunity to become one." Which I am not, I hasten to add.

He looked at me thoughtfully, and then raised a slight smile. But I was right. It was up to me to prove myself. If I had been a failure he would have had little hesitation in sacking me. It was the start of Roy Waller.

listeners with me. Much of that world would be live and real, but some of it would be make believe.

I drew on my boyhood memories when I experimented with my reel-to-reel tape recorder and created sound effects – those Waller reports that drove my family mad. On radio the listener cannot see exactly what you are doing in the studio, so that you can use sound effects to make the audience believe something is going on when it isn't – this after all is the essence of drama. I came up with some crazy items. I used sound effects to convey knitting and then welding. The listeners thought I must be pretty good at both, though I am sure they enjoyed the click-click of the knitting needles more than the jarring notes of what I cooked up as a welding machine. I then ventured into a dungeon, creating sound effects that sounded really scary and a lot better than those you find in some amusement parks. People rang in expressing concern, and the hope that I would manage to escape; they thought that it was all for real.

I became more ambitious. I was out in the countryside for a walk one day when I saw a magnificent hot air balloon soaring above. I could hear its blowers ignite enabling it to rise higher as the passengers gazed down on the Norfolk landscape. Couldn't I pretend to be in a hot air balloon over Norwich, I wondered? My imagination ran away with me; I could pilot the balloon and land on the roof of Norfolk Towers. That would be a good wheeze. With the help of the magnificent BBC sound archives, I put together a tape on ballooning, with sound effects ranging from the swishing of the air to the roar of the igniting burners.

When I aired this story it caused a bit of a stir. I told listeners that I was up in a hot air balloon heading for Norwich to present my programme. I said I planned to land on the roof of Norfolk Towers. Soon there were quite a few people in the streets below peering upwards to see if they could spot me. Ensconced in my studio, playing the tape, I chuckled to myself. But then the commissionaire from the front reception of the building, which belonged to Norwich Union, came rushing into the Radio Norfolk manager's office shouting: "He can't do that! He can't do that! He needs permission to land on the roof."

"What are you on about?" the manager asked the jobsworth from downstairs.

The commissionaire explained that Waller had just said on his programme that he was about to descend upon the roof of this least attractive corner of the Norwich Union empire, adding that his bosses would be extremely angry as it was a clear breach of the health and safety regulations.

"It's news to me," the manager said, "I thought he was in the studio."

The commissionaire was shown to my studio, where a production assistant pointed me out. It is not recorded exactly what the man in uniform said, but I do not think he found my stunt amusing.

I also used to fake wind-up calls live on air. I love mimicking different voices and accents, and have caught people out more than once. Of all the hundreds of wind-ups that I have done I have only had two calls where people have used foul language. My boss used to get very nervous about these live calls and tried to persuade me to pre-record them. But this part of the afternoon show proved very popular with listeners, and he gave in.

People would write in and recommend someone for a wind-up phone call, and this led me to impersonate people from many walks of life. I remember once catching out the Chief Inspector from Diss, and he said that one day he would pay me back. I did not take much notice of this, as I am ex-directory at home, and all my calls at Radio Norfolk are filtered. However, he caught me out when I least expected it, and it was not April 1 either.

I was recording my afternoon programme when David Clayton walked in with a uniformed policeman. The officer read out a statement, and said he was going to arrest me. He produced a pair of handcuffs and marched me out of the studio. I thought it was a joke, but began to worry then when I saw the squad car outside. The next thing I knew, he had dipped my head and bundled me into the back of the vehicle. The police officer got into the back of the car with me and said to the driver: "Take over, take him to Bethel Street." By that time I was in a fair old panic, and I said to the driver: "I know the Chief Inspector at Diss; please contact him." The driver turned around to me and said "Gotcha." I suppose it was bound to happen one day.

I remember on one programme I rang up a chap and, from the conversation that followed, realised that he had no teeth in. I asked him about his lack of teeth, and he said that his wife had taken them because she was concerned about his cholesterol level. I was a bit bemused by this but he then explained that he was addicted to walnuts, but without his teeth he could not eat them. I asked him why she did not hide the nuts instead, and he said it was because he always used to find them, whereas he could never find his teeth! This went out live on air but he didn't know who I was. The funny thing was that the next day I rang him again and he said that some bloke had heard about him on the radio yesterday. "How did they find that out?" he asked.

These were the things I used to get up to. Then the time came when I found I needed someone to bounce ideas off, and preferably someone who could come on air and react to some of the things I was saying, such as my knitting or welding! There was a personable girl in the BBC offices called Sylvie, and the management

Roy with Dolores – or is it Sylvie?

assigned her to work with me.

I did not much like the name of Sylvie, and told them so. They said I could call her what I liked, and I cringe when I recall that poor Sylvie had very little say in the matter. I was reading a novel at the time with a character in it called Dolores, a South American prostitute. I thought it was a fantastic name. So Sylvie became known as Dolores, and was introduced as such on the radio.

My assistant later became my girl-friend and eventually my wife. These days Sylvie is embarrassed when people meet us and are not sure whether she is Dolores or Sylvie. She manages to contain herself, and says politely: "My name is not Dolores." And she cringes as I explain the story of how I gave her that name.

Sylvie liked being on the radio, although this caused a bit of an upset at Radio Norfolk. In those days it was not usual for production assistants to go on air. In fact, more than that, it was frowned upon. I could not see the problem: frequently we had guests on air with Norfolk accents and untrained voices, and Sylvie had a good voice. I was told not to let her broadcast, but I ignored the instruction. They said, "You cannot do that," and I retorted, "Yes I can."

Eventually they relented for a trial period. Sylvie was nervous at first, but very successful. I never told her what we were going to do, and every one of my yarns started off with a sound effect. I just wanted her to react naturally and impulsively to what I said. Sylvie was wonderful. She had a very infectious laugh, and she would giggle at what I said, and come up with a spontaneous reaction. The listeners loved it, and soon she was getting her own fan mail. The management liked that, and it was not long before they accepted that Sylvie could play a role on the microphone as well as off it.

The natural corollary to having an adult on the show was to introduce children. So I invented Sebastian and Oliver, and used the BBC sound archive to make them sound real. I would play with these imaginary children on air, scold them, joke with them, and show them conjuring tricks. We would take them down to the dungeon, and hear their "ooos" and "ahs". The listeners took Sebastian and Oliver to their hearts. At Christmas time they even sent them cards and presents, which Dolores and I would then distribute to needy children in children's homes.

When Dolores was away on holiday or unwell I had another woman to help out, called Roxy. I introduced Roxy as the mother of my children, and part-time helper when my production assistant could not be there. The audience thought it was true.

This inspired me to create more characters, mostly using listeners who rang in. A man rang up one day and said he was painting the Sydney Harbour Bridge, but he kept dropping his paint brush. I talked to him about it on air, and he became a regular on the programme once or twice a week chatting about his painting. Then one day I was shocked to receive a call from his wife. She told me that her husband was really a house painter and decorator. "You have got to stop this nonsense," she said. "I cannot get him out of the house to do any work because he always wants to be talking with you." He was a lovely character, but I did not want to be responsible for him losing work and perhaps even his marriage. I decided I had to drop him.

Soon my afternoon programme was to take another leap into the world of fantasy. I had watched a compelling series about the SAS on BBC Television, and was intrigued. I mentioned it on my programme, and then added: "Of course I was in the SAS, but I am not allowed to talk about it."

But I needed characters. At about this time I went on a BBC listeners' trip to Austria. I went up a mountain in a cable car, and as we climbed through the forest I spotted a mountain goat perched precariously on a ledge. I said to a woman companion: "Gosh, I wonder how he got there?" and, quick as a flash, she replied, "By mountain bike, of course."

I decided I could use that kind of wit on air. So I chatted to the woman and when we got back to Norfolk I christened her Saggy Sandra, and introduced her as a member of the SAS. I told listeners Saggy and I had to go off on special training high in the Austrian Tyrol. In real life she lived on the royal estate at Sandringham with her husband, who was a tractor driver for the Queen. When people there recognised her voice and realised that she was the radio character they started to call her Saggy as well, though that was not her real name.

Then I started to look for more characters. There was Micky X, whom I also met on a listeners' trip. He worked in Cambridge, and had a great sense of humour. I put him on quite a bit, whenever he rang up in fact, because we had such a good rapport. Another character was Wimpy Barry, so called because he did not like the sight of blood or some of the things the SAS get up to. He had first got in touch with us because he came up with good ideas for competitions.

Then the BBC's Norwich office accountant told me, "I love your SAS," and suggested I introduce some kind of effeminate person. "What a good idea," I said, "I must look out for someone." "I will do it for you," he volunteered. And so he did, and always managed to sound a bit camp. I christened him Bubbly Bertie, and he had a boyfriend called Chase Me Chedson.

The SAS, of course, formed only a small part of the afternoon show, but it was the one that gave me the most fun. It certainly did not give me any trouble, unlike the occasion when I decided to create Billy, the building's security man, as an on-air character. Billy really wanted to be a radio presenter, and would make it plain that he thought he could do a better job than most of those who were employed in that capacity, including me. On my programme, he took the mickey out of all of us.

By this time I was well established. People outside the BBC were talking about Roy Waller, and I found doors opening for me. I would be invited to open fetes and shops. The latter was sometimes a mixed blessing. I once went to open a bridal gown shop in Wisbech, and they asked me if I would get into a wedding gown to have my picture taken. "No way," I said, so they pinned a dress on me and photographed that.

I also began being asked to compere live shows. My first was at the Theatre Royal in Norwich, and although I had plenty of experience by then I was terrified. I was, and am, a fairly shy person in public. My mother, when told I would be doing this, said immediately, "That's not my Roy; he would not do that."

She probably remembered when my father died, and I was expected to stand up at his wake and speak. I simply could not do it. I kept breaking down. Afterwards David Clayton, my managing editor said to me, "You know Roy, if I had given you a microphone, it would have been no problem." He is quite right. Put a microphone in my hand and the shyness disappears.

Sylvie Waller with Daniel O'Donnell

And so it was at the Theatre Royal. There were 1400 people in the audience as I walked on stage, and the spotlight was upon me. I told a joke, but I was so nervous that I delivered the punch line first. I then said, "Sorry ladies and gentlemen, this is the first time I have ever compered a show, can I tell the joke properly?" They said "yes", and so I did, and they laughed, bless them.

Once I had gained more experience I really enjoyed compering shows. The BBC also came to realise they could hang an audience on me. They sent me off to the Royal Norfolk Show, where I presented my programme, and did a live stage show as well. I pulled in a good audience, and we were in full swing when the Queen passed by. Instantly, I instructed the crowd to turn round and wave to her, which they did. Perhaps I should be "By Royal Appointment", because the Queen has attended my afternoon show.

I loved having children on the programme, and the phrase "What's for tea, mother?" was a favourite with them. The answer was often sausages though occasionally it was roast beef. Sometimes you had to think fast. I asked a young boy once, "Where's your mother?" and got the reply, "She's in the cemetery." I could have fallen in the trap of saying "I am so sorry." But dealing with the bereaved has taught me not to wallow in pity, so I said, "I bet your father looks after you well," and the boy said: "My Dad gives me everything."

I was once sitting on a tropical beach 5000 miles from Britain when a voice said, "What's for tea, mother?" I looked up and a listener from Wymondham introduced himself. In radio, there is no escape from the audience, and I like it that way.

I feel a bond with the audience, and I think many listeners share that feeling. I once said on air, "I've got troubles down below." I was just fooling about, for there was nothing wrong with me,

but people did not know that. They could speculate, of course. Some thought it was an in-growing toe nail; others believed it was something more serious. Then I received a letter from the matron at the Norfolk and Norwich Hospital, who thanked me for "highlighting the problem of people who have troubles down below". She said that until I mentioned the subject people would not talk about these problems. And people would stop me in the streets, or in shops and whisper their commiserations to me. It was not until I went to the United States about 18 months ago that I told listeners, "You will be pleased to know I went private. I have now had my troubles down below done, and they are in a jam jar in my home."

There was one day that I actually thought that I had died on air. I was doing the afternoon show with Sylvie when suddenly the whole studio went dark. I couldn't see or hear a thing. I heard my voice saying "Sylvie", but there was no response at all. I thought, "Roy, your time is up and you are moving on." Then after an eternity I heard a familiar voice saying "Roy". I said, "Sylvie, thank goodness it's you, I thought I had died."

Recently I have been moved to the morning programme, and it is a different Roy Waller for a different time of day. I have not transferred my characters to the new show, because that would not work. People miss them, and have told me they wish I was still on air in the afternoon. But that's gone now, and I am planning on revamping the mornings, and I am enjoying it. I introduced "Hairy Legs Day", and the phones lit up with women calling in and saying they did not know there was such an occasion, but they were shaving their legs. I asked people to tell me what music they would play at their funeral, and there was a huge response.

People often ask me if is there anybody whom I would really like to interview on my show. There are two. There is the outstanding Arsenal manager, Arsène Wenger, whom I admire for the way he approaches football, and for his remarkable skill in man management. And the Queen. The monarchy has always fascinated me. I have been told that the afternoon show was on a radio in the stables at Sandringham House when I said: "I believe that the Queen is staying at Sandringham at the moment, I hope you are enjoying your holiday ma'am." At that point, so I was told, she went up to the set and said "Having a lovely time, thank you very much!"

I had the pleasure of meeting Prince Phillip at Sandringham. He was charming. He came up to me and said: "You are the football chap," and we had a conversation about a certain player.

Of all the listeners' trips I have taken the most memorable was in June 2001 when I did not create any new characters, but came home with a new bride. Sylvie and I did not intend to get married when we escorted a group of listeners to the Pacific coast of the United States and western Canada. We were quite happy as we were. We had been to Vancouver, and then travelled on a cruise ship through Victoria Sound and up towards the Rocky Mountains. I asked the captain if there were ever wedding ceremonies on board. He nodded, and said "Yes" very positively. So I asked him, "Will you marry me?"

His face fell. "Me, marry you?" he replied.

"No, no, not marry me! I want you to marry Sylvie and I."

He looked sheepish, "I have never conducted a marriage before. So, no, I won't," he said.

This turn of events took Sylvie completely by surprise. I had not told her of my plan, and as she sat looking at us her mouth dropped open. I think she thought it was one of my stunts. So I then proposed to her, "Will you marry me?" I asked. "Well, yes," she said.

Although we had been dating for a long time, I had never raised the subject of marriage before, but on this boat trip I suddenly realised that this was the way to do it. Romantic. Far from home and routine, relatives and all that.

The captain told us that if we left the ship at the next stop, Kamloops, and stayed there for two nights we could legally get married under Canadian law. Kamloops was a lovely place, in the interior of British Columbia, a town surrounded by lakes and mountains. It has an exciting Wild West history that includes the fur trade, gold rush and cattle ranching. Close by is Canada's biggest cattle ranch. There could not be a better place for a couple that likes country music.

"What about the family?" Sylvie asked, but I said, "Don't worry, we'll tell them, and we will have a blessing and a big party when we get back." So three days later, in the honeymoon suite of the Stockman's Hotel we were married by a local vicar. Saggy Sandra was a witness, and great bouquets of flowers arrived from Norfolk, via Interflora.

Then we went down to tell the rest of the Radio Norfolk listeners. "Sylvie and I," I said, remembering this time not to call her Dolores, "are now man and wife." They did not believe it. They thought it was another one of my jokes. There were quite a few Japanese guests in this hotel, so we invited them to join us for a reception. I introduced them to the Birdie Song, to the delight of the Norfolk group. By this time everyone realised it was for real, and we had a great evening. We enjoyed another great party in Norfolk in the September of that year after our church blessing.

Chapter 6
Carrow Road

I love winter Saturdays at Carrow Road. The fans streaming across Carrow bridge to the ground, all well-padded against the cold wind that often comes from the east, and sporting their yellow and green woolly scarves and hats. There are the cries of the programme sellers, the whiff of sizzling hamburgers and sausages coming from stalls, and the clink of the turnstiles as Norwich City attracts yet another full house. Not for us the bare terraces and forlorn grounds of teams that perhaps once tasted glory, but who now struggle to attract just a few thousand spectators. I always felt sad going to watch games against Wimbledon, when they were still at Selhurst Park in south London. It is a huge ground, but there were always several times more empty spaces than Dons' supporters, who were usually outnumbered by the Canary faithful.

The crowd and the atmosphere are not just about being in the Premiership. Even during some of Norwich City's less successful seasons in Division One, there has always been a buzz about Carrow Road on a Saturday. Norfolk people love their football. Supporters feel that they are coming to *their* club. They belong. Much of the

credit for this atmosphere is due to the supporters themselves. They have an outstanding reputation for loyalty through good times and bad. But the club management has also done an excellent job in creating a good environment. There is the new South Stand, which somehow has amplified the noise from the fans and was built as an act of faith when Norwich's return to the top flight of soccer was far from certain. Many sponsorships and side activities have grown with the help of our former goalkeeping hero, Bryan Gunn. Much improved catering has blossomed under the influence of Delia Smith. We treat our visitors well. Away supporters coming to Carrow Road appreciate the facilities at the ground, which is not like the inhospitable places we often encounter on our travels, where sometimes it is difficult to get even a cup of tea.

But, of course, these days Saturday is a workday, and a long day at that. Inevitably much of it is routine. I get up early, just as I do between Mondays and Fridays, and drive in to the Forum, where BBC Radio Norfolk is now based. Unlike weekdays I dress down, turning up in my tracksuit and trainers. But I carry a tote bag with a change of

The players warm up at Carrow Road before the last Division 1 game against Preston

clothing, because when I do my commentaries I always like to wear a suit and tie. I think it is important to be well dressed when in places like the directors' room.

My first job is always to present my country music programme, which runs from nine until midday. I will have done most of the preparation beforehand, but there are always details which need tidying up, guests to look after and interview. You have to be on the ball because in radio it is easy to make mistakes if you are careless and not concentrating. I owe it to the listeners to focus on what I am broadcasting, so I banish completely all thoughts of football and the approaching game, even if it is against Arsenal or Manchester United.

When I am off air at midday, I head for the ladies' toilet, and change into my suit. I do not make a practice of this, but there are no women around at this time. There is more room, and the facilities are much better. The BBC obviously believes that their male staff do not need to preen in front of a mirror!

Suitably spruced up, I pick up my clipboard and bits and pieces and head for the sports desk; Saturday is their biggest day. I have a brief chat with the sports editor, exchanging views about the afternoon's game. Quite often he will request an interview with a particular player, or suggest an angle he would like covered. Sometimes he may ask for additional interviews after the game. I then meet up with our technical man, Bobby Castleton, and we head off to Carrow Road.

Normally David Clayton, head of BBC Radio Norfolk, picks us up and we drive down to the ground together. There is always some banter with the steward at the main car park, who is very careful about whom he lets in. On one occasion David joked to him, "I have got some celebrities in the back, including a very special one." I looked around and asked David, "Who is coming? Anyone I know?" The car park man said, "Oh, it's only Roy is it! You'd better park over there then." He always finds us a nice parking spot.

As we walk the hundred yards or so to the City Stand, I invariably spend time chatting to fans who have come down to the ground early. They stop me, and ask questions about the game and my score predictions, about which I am usually cautious. Sometimes I am asked to sign autographs or people's shirts, and I joke that my playing days are over.

Eventually I make it to the main entrance making a point of shaking hands with the stewards. These are key people in any football club, good blokes who have an important job to do, and who can be very helpful if they know you. I have a chat with Val, the receptionist behind the main desk, who is the first point of contact for visitors to Norwich City.

I pick up the keys to our commentary box, and head upstairs where there is more banter with the guys who hand out programmes. The Norwich City programme *On the Ball*, edited by Peter Rogers, is one of the best around. It was the Nationwide programme of the year in 2003, and is certainly up in the top ten. On our promotion to the Premiership, a 100-page souvenir edition was published and is definitely a collector's item.

Bobby and I go into our BBC studio just next to the directors' room. I leave my clipboard and game notes there, and make my way through the directors' room and other parts of the club, chatting for a moment or two with people I know.

Invariably I bump into the referee and his officials, sitting munching their lunchtime sandwiches with a cup of tea, and watching a live game on Sky Sports television. What did they do before Sky, I wonder? I'll say, "Good afternoon, gentlemen, good to see you all," and they will say, "Nice to see you: how are you?" Sometimes as I walk away I will say to my companion, with a grin, "I could not see his white stick and guide dog," and out of the corner of my eye watch for their reaction. Just a little joke.

My destination is the Gunn Club. The club is a marvellous institution run by the former Norwich and Scotland goalkeeping legend, Bryan Gunn, high up in the Barclay stand. Those who have joined the club come in and have lunch there before home games. Both at lunchtime and after the game Bryan gives his views, and people can have a drink and relax. After the game some of the players will turn up.

I sit down for lunch, usually interrupted many times by people coming over for a chat. I don't mind that; it's enjoyable, and lunch is not formal. David Clayton will offer to buy me a glass of red wine, but I decline because if I have a couple of glasses I have difficulty in remembering the players' names, something Neil Adams will not let me forget.

I rarely have time to eat the dessert, I am too busy talking, and, because I am the official host when Bryan is busy elsewhere, I have to make a little speech introducing visitors and welcoming them to Carrow Road. Sometimes Delia will come over and ask me to have a chat to a VIP guest on her table: she almost always has lunch in the Gunn Club.

Some time before two o'clock I leave the club and return to the studio where Chris Goreham will be preparing to host his sports programme. He may have heard of an interesting visitor who has arrived to see the match – a former Norwich star perhaps, or a sporting personality – and will ask me if I can try and find him and persuade him to come up to our studio for an interview.

I will go down to the dressing room, and grab a cup of tea from the tea lady – I have no idea what her name is because everyone, including me, calls her "mother". Captain Canary and Splat the Cat will be hanging around, and I will give them my joke of the day just as they are trying to get into their uniforms and take to the pitch.

With or without an interviewee, I go back upstairs, and chat with Chris on air live for about 20 minutes. We discuss the team Nigel Worthington has picked, the opposition, and the prospects for the 90 minutes that are fast approaching.

Then I go to the commentary box and meet up with Neil Adams, who is my summarizer. When I take a short pause in my commentary, perhaps because the ball is out of play or someone is injured, or I need to get my breath back, he jumps in with sensible or not-so-sensible comments. Occasionally he repeats what I have just said, which must annoy the listeners, but most of the time his comments are excellent and enlightening, the kind of thing you would expect from a former top-notch professional footballer who never seemed to miss a penalty when he played for Norwich.

He will have been given the latest team news, and will set out the expected formation on a piece of paper we keep in front of us, with the shirt numbers against each name. Down below us the players will have trickled out of the tunnel for their warm-up exercises, and will be going through their warm-up before going back to the dressing room for a change of kit and a final briefing from Nigel.

Then it is time for my major physical exercise of the day – clambering into the commentary box. I have to lift myself over the top and jump in, much to the amusement of the crowd who probably think I will not make it. When he was chairman, Robert Chase promised that a proper door would be provided, but it was never done.

Once I have sat down and established myself, I am reminded I am among friends. There are broad Norfolk accents everywhere, that distinctive dialect that still can be heard throughout our county despite the infusion of outsiders. Over the years I have come to know the people who sit near the commentary box – there are a lady and gentleman on my right, both well-travelled, and if they are not there then their son turns up with his friend. Then there's John from Bawburgh Golf Club, and many others, who all wave to me and ask what I think will be the score. I usually just say 2-1 and leave it at that. It's like that throughout the ground. When I used to go as a spectator to the old South Stand it was "Hello Roy, hello John, hello Fred." A friendly place.

At five to three there is a crackle in my ear, and they say, "Roy, we are coming to you in 20 seconds," and off we go. First I set the scene, and then there is a roar as the players come out of the tunnel, with the Norwich boys always turning right towards the Norwich and Peterborough stand. Neil will chip in some thoughts, and by this time the players have lined up, and the game kicks off.

The first 45 minutes fly by, and unless someone is injured there is little pause for breath. Delivering a radio live commentary is, I think, much harder than television, where you do not have to fill all the air time with talk, you can let the pictures speak for themselves, particularly with set-pieces. In radio you have to create word pictures of everything you see, and, of course, you must name the players as the ball passes from one to another. This is easy enough with the Norwich team, because I know them all, but it is more difficult with the visitors, particularly these days when so many footballers have come from overseas. It is essential to get pronunciation right, you cannot say Lulu when the striker's name (Lua Lua) is phonetically Loo-Ah Loo-Ah.

Of course I prepare thoroughly. I have notes on my clipboard about players' backgrounds, but nothing like BBC Television's John Motson, who seems to be able to recall every goal and every incident a player has been involved in over the years. He is a

Michael looks on as Delia talks up Norwich City

walking encyclopedia of football knowledge.

No one looks forward to the half-time whistle more than Neil Adams. The second the whistle is blown he is out of the commentary box like a greyhound on the starting traps. He does not want to make it into the boardroom only to find the best cookies have been scoffed. So he is up and running and in there grabbing a handful of biscuits before we even arrive. By the time I get there I am at the end of a long tea queue. I chat with Delia and Michael, Duncan Forbes, Dave Stringer or some of the others as together we watch the other half-time scores come over the television. Often my friend Bruce Rioch will be there – even as an ex-manager he is welcome at Carrow Road. That is one of the special things about the club. Old employees are not shut out, but treated with dignity and warmth.

I finish my tea and climb back in to the commentary box. Neil is already there, having gobbled all the biscuits, and off we go again. At the end of the match when the final whistle is blown Neil is off again, but this time heading for the studio where he hosts a post match phone-in programme that is very popular. I stay put, and write a considered piece about the game, which is run in our sports round up. While I am doing this the players will be jogging out for their warm-down. I will exchange some banter with some of them, usually Malky Mackay and Craig Fleming. I might say to Craig on the rare occasion he scores a goal, "Was it a 50 yard dash and a diving header?" and he will say, "Oh, 60 yards at least," when it was probably just a tap-in. I will then record my written summary, always ending with the final score.

Television might want a piece from me, but usually no longer than 25 seconds. It is hard to cram a lot of goals into 25 seconds, but if I run over time they will insist I do it again at the length they have prescribed. Then it is down to the dressing room on the ground floor of the main stand where I hang around with the other journalists. Invariably the door will open and Nigel will come out first. He nearly always gives me the first interview, and if someone else tries to jump in first he points to me and says, "No, I do that man over there." I will ask questions for a couple of minutes, and then say, "Thank you Nigel for joining us." The others pick up from there, although more often than not they will use my

Postcard from the BBC

recording but chop out my questions and replace them with their own.

Then I wait for a player to emerge from the dressing room on his way to the players' lounge. I usually want to interview a goal scorer or the "man of the match", and sometimes need two. For instance, if Robert Green has made a spectacular save I will go for him. It can be a long wait.

Some of the players change quickly and leave, without giving us the opportunity to approach them. Many do not go to the players' lounge. Perhaps they are going out with their wives or girlfriends, or have another engagement, or simply do not wish to socialize. I might say to Joe (Joe Ferrari, the Norwich press relations manager), "Any chance of speaking with Paul McVeigh?" and the reply will come, "He's gone." Paul is one of those players who will answer a question with a question. He can be cheeky. This is typical:

WALLER: Paul, that was a great goal.
MCVEIGH: Did you see the goal, Roy?
WALLER: Yes, I did. It was your sixth
          goal this season.
MCVEIGH: You can count then?

I can only be thankful that he doesn't assist me in the commentary box. When I went to the civic reception at City Hall I said to him, " You gave me a hard time", and he said, "You deserve it."

Craig Fleming is another one who gives me stick, and I give it back. We both enjoy jousting. Malky Mackay speculated whether my relationship with the players would be different in the Premiership, but concluded it would still be good because, as he said, "You are on our side." And I am. I see the game through yellow and green spectacles, and make no apologies for that.

When he was at the club, Iwan Roberts was another player who liked to get off home quickly. He would go into the main reception and wait there for his wife and children, and then be off. If I wanted to speak with him I would have to go to the front door and intercept him there.

I take my recorder upstairs and the boys feed the interviews to our Forum headquarters. And that's it. If I am going out I walk back to the Forum, pick up my car, and drive home. Sometimes I have an evening engagement, and I have to put on another suit and compere a show, a dinner or some other event. That will take me right up to midnight. But I prefer not to do that on a Saturday. It will have been a long day, and I prefer to go home and relax in front of the television.

In the season there is also a lot of travelling, once a fortnight to be precise, and sometimes more often. That means I have to record my country music programme on a Friday afternoon, because most of Norwich's away fixtures require a fair old journey. There's only one short trip, to Ipswich Town's Portman Road, and hopefully we will not be going there for a while.

With the exception of games against London clubs, most away fixtures involve four or five hours on the road. Three of us go, and we share the driving, always leaving Norwich very early so as to get to our destination in good time. As a broadcaster I cannot be late. I like to allow plenty of time to familiarize myself with the ground, the team sheet, and to pick up any news and gossip from the players and others from the club.

Sometimes Neil and I argue about the amount of time we allow to get anywhere, but my AA experiences taught me to play safe. Road trips usually mean a traffic jam somewhere, as well as ice, snow and fog on winter mornings. We can prepare for that but not for cattle on the motorway, as happened on the way to Old Trafford for the game against Manchester United in August 2004.

Most of the clubs we visit are hospitable, particularly ones with which we have a good relationship, such as Sunderland or Arsenal. Chelsea used to be interesting because Norwich has had a love-hate relationship with the former chairman Ken Bates. He admired Norwich, and especially the way we look after disabled supporters, and I remember him taking a walk past the Norwich and Peterborough stand,

from where fans goaded him, to inspect the facility. But he also thought Norwich had sold him two duds in Robert Fleck and Chris Sutton. He could not understand why players who scored freely for Norwich could not find the net for Chelsea. It will be interesting to visit Stamford Bridge under its new ownership: Neil is hoping they will pass round a vodka bottle at half-time – with the biscuits, of course.

It has to be said that the facilities at some clubs are terrible. Neil and I always take a blanket with us, because it can be freezing. If we were staying in the First Division I think I might invest in a cushion. Some clubs seem reluctant to rustle up a cup of tea for the commentators. Others must have heard of Neil's reputation because they hide the biscuit barrel.

You see some strange sights at away grounds. At Deepdale, the ground of Preston North End, I saw a man taking his dog for a walk during the game. Believe me, there was not a lamppost within sight, and I found myself distracted from what was happening on the pitch because I could imagine the dog might find an alternative. You sometimes also see dogs on the pitch, though how they get there I do not know.

I once went to Cambridge, where there are allotments between the stadium and the pitch. When the game became tedious you felt like breaking into a commentary about how well old Tom's shallots were doing, or about the caterpillars eating the cabbages.

At Oxford United about ten of us were encased in a glass box, and my equipment caught fire as I was reporting. I flapped at it, but carried on talking, while several of the reporters ran out shouting "Fire, Fire" which sounded strange on air. We put it out, but I had to ring BBC Radio Oxford and borrow some equipment.

Port Vale in the Potteries was an interesting place; I am not sorry we do not go there any more. You had to climb up on to the roof of the stand, as the wind whistled around. There was an old shed, and when you opened the door you half expected to find a lawn mower inside. In fact, what you discovered was another radio commentator, from the Port Vale side. It was impossible to work in the same shed, so I had to go outside and try and find a duffle coat with a good hood.

We went to Swansea for the FA Cup, and they made us shin up a pole with the help of a small ladder. I could not climb the pole and carry my equipment at the same time, so they rigged up a rope and hoisted it up to me. At the top of the pole there were some iron railings, and I hurt my back as I leaned over to grab the equipment. Groaning with pain, I staggered into my commentary position, and reported the game. By the second half I was in agony, but could do nothing about it. Afterwards I took my shirt off and found bloody grazes and heavy bruising.

Fortunately, I do not often have to interview managers of teams we visit. Most of them are not like Nigel who, as I have said, is straightforward and honest. He will always be interviewed win or lose. He will never criticize his players, individually or collectively, but equally will not try to hide his disappointment if they have not played well.

Some managers are irascible. Gary Megson is the one I try to avoid. Sir Alex Ferguson has his moments too. I do not know exactly what happened in the dressing room incident in 2003 with Beckham, but I know he can be irritable. I once asked him why his players were so intimidating. "What kind of f***ing question is that?" he snorted, and stomped off.

In football we do occasionally have trouble with the F word, which of course is proscribed by BBC Radio. When he was playing for Norwich but out of action through injury, Keith O'Neill had a run as my summarizer, and would break out into coarse language. "What kind of f***ing foul was that?" he'd shout at the referee and into the microphone at the same time. I had to try and cover it and told him to mind his language. Another problem with Keith was that he would get into a conversation with spectators near us, and talk to them about his injuries, all of which went out on air.

Yet he was better than one player who did a stint with me, and just repeated everything I said. If I reported:

Roy interviews Mike Walker when he was manager

Robert Chase signs Roy as cover for Bryan Gunn. The lads look apprehensive

'I think he is going to hit it to the right'

"Yes, I think he was offside," he would say: "Yes, I think he was offside." He drove me mad.

Matt Jackson was good fun, and I was sad when he fell out of favour. Matt had an excellent sense of humour and would play tricks on me. He referred to one of the players as "Fluffy", and told me that was his name. So later in the game I too referred to the player as "Fluffy", and at the end of the match asked Matt where the player acquired the nickname. "I made it up," Matt said.

Neil Adams suits me very well. He reads my mind, and complements my commentary. He is clever and articulate, and does not criticize players needlessly. In his phone-in programme after the game he will not go along with listeners who attack players. He also thinks about our comforts. When we went to Milton Keynes for the Wimbledon game he took a blanket and a borrowed heater from the press room, and it got so hot I had to pass a note to him to turn the wretched thing off.

I try not to work on a Sunday. Every second weekend during the winter I will have had a long drive back from an away game, perhaps from a place as far away as Newcastle or Manchester, so I do not get up early on Sunday mornings.

I have a lie-in, with breakfast in bed, reading the Sunday papers until about 10.30. The paper I like best is the *Mail on Sunday*. However if Norwich has lost the previous day I tend not to read the match report, as it will depress me. For the rest of the day I will do nothing, unless there is a fete to open or a Norfolk event I have agreed to attend, or, of course a match at Carrow Road. What I like best about Sundays is watching football on Sky. If I can, I will just flop in the chair and watch all three live games from beginning to end. It is perfect relaxation. And then I might go to bed at half past eight, to recharge the batteries for the week ahead.

Chapter 7
Canary Managers

If you cover the games and behind-the-scenes activities of a major football club for your local radio station, meeting with and reporting on the actions of the manager is an essential part of everyday life. Over the years I have come to know most of Norwich City's managers well, and some of them I count among my friends.

One of the toughest was the first with whom I had to deal: Ron Saunders. Ron was very much the hard man. It was an image he rather enjoyed; certainly he did very little to dispel it. In particular he felt his prime responsibility was to get his players fit, and for him the best way to do that was to make them run them up to the top of Mousehold. Some players were physically sick. Saunders' regime was like tough army training, where he would instill into them the fact that they had to exercise until they dropped. Yet he always led by example, stripping off his shirt and running up and down the steep slopes with them. Ron was a hard taskmaster compared with most present day coaches, but he was convinced that this regime was the way to build up leg muscles and to keep the players running for the full 90 minutes of league matches.

Sometimes he took it to extremes, for example by making the players head medicine balls, which would not be allowed these days. But many of his team are still alive to tell the tale, and do not seem to have been brain damaged.

Ron did not suffer fools gladly, or those who disagreed with him publicly. He would throw reporters off the team coach and leave them stranded at away grounds. Often the local press travelled on the coach to be close to the action, and to save their news organisations' money. But if he felt journalists were undermining his authority he would order them off the coach. A reporter who felt he might upset Ron by what he said or wrote would take the return train fare with him as insurance for getting home.

Yet it is interesting that very few players went against him; those that did quickly found themselves out of favour and cast into the wilderness. His tough approach was very evident both on the pitch and in the dressing room. If you were a player you had no choice but to comply. He brought the best out of the players, but only by bullying them. He would shout at them from the touchline, naming them personally. They respected him for his honesty, and his ability to turn them into better players.

Press conferences were exactly the same. He would tell you in no uncertain terms what he thought, and if you disagreed he did not care. He was not going to change his mind. Keith Skipper recalls when he was covering Norwich City for the *Eastern Evening News* he telephoned the football club to check something for a story. He was put through to the office and made a remark about the manager's team selection. The voice at the other end abruptly said, "This is Ron Saunders and I do not care what you think," and banged the phone down. Keith was very embarrassed, but left in no doubt as to who was boss.

In retrospect I think he was a good manager, but in the end he moved on to better himself. You cannot blame him for that. Each manager wants to improve his career. Ron comes back to Norwich City reunions, and his former players, like Duncan Forbes, still remember him as the "hard man". Duncan himself was pretty tough, but he will remind you that in his long career he was never once sent off. He went on to become the club's chief scout, and is still a fine ambassador for the Canaries. Duncan is a great character, known for his non-stop shouting on the pitch of his great saying, "Keep your voice down to a roar." These days he will tell you all about the important signings he made, but keeps quiet about the bad ones.

Duncan travelled a great deal as chief scout, especially when Bruce Rioch was manager. They often went scouting together. There is a lovely story Bruce tells about Duncan. Forbes always carried a bag of humbugs, but on the car journey to watch a player he would ration Bruce to one mint on the way out, and one for the return journey. Never more, no matter how long the trip.

After Saunders came John Bond,

Bruce and Jane Rioch with Roy out West

who was a very colourful character, and a complete contrast to Ron. He was very much the man with glitter: he wore fine jewellery and designer clothes. His suits were well cut, and teamed with beautiful shirts. John would breeze into the dressing room, jewellery jangling, but he did have an ability to inspire people. He had a glamorous image, and was often surrounded by his support staff, including Mel Machin and Ken Brown. Mel, who went on to manage other clubs, was a brilliant coach, and John took advantage of that.

Particularly memorable was John's decision to bring his son into the club. Kevin, who at that stage was a gangly player, seemed to many to have little potential. We used to look at him and think, "No, he will never make it as a footballer," but John would say in that lovely voice of his, "You just watch my boy, he's fantastic." We all thought he was having us on. Bond played his son at full back and Kevin became a stalwart of defence, and later followed his father into coaching.

John Bond spent more time with the media than in training. He would amble on to the training ground, which was then at Trowse, and stand in the middle of the pitch and look pensive. There would be lots of activity, but he would just kick a few balls about with the players, and then slope off to conduct an interview. Yet he had this wonderful charisma which made you think he should not really be a football manager, but a showbiz celebrity. Everyone respected John Bond, he was a good manager and he brought in stars like Charlie Boyer and Ted McDougall. Both of them liked him so much they followed him whenever he moved on.

When John Bond left, Ken Brown was his deputy, and the chairman at the time, Robert Chase, gave him the chance to take over. Brown had earlier been a Norwich player, and before that he had played at West Ham, and so he was familiar with the passing game that was the hallmark of Norwich City. Ken was a likeable guy and good in the dressing room, but also sensitive to criticism. One day I was down at Trowse, and I heard a voice bawling behind me. I looked round and it was Ken, and rather to my surprise it appeared he was shouting at me. I raised my eyebrows and he shouted, "Yes, you!"

He said, "I didn't like what you said at the last home game on the radio."

Dave Stringer: 'abused in the street'

Ken had his favourites. He worked very well with a reporter who came from Eastern Counties Newspapers, now known as Archant. Ken would invite him to the dressing room and leave us all outside in the cold. If he wanted to do that there was nothing we could do to stop him.

Brown's successor was another former player, Dave Stringer, one of the few managers who was Norfolk-born; he came from Gorleston. Dave was manager for five years and spent all this time in the top flight until his departure.

When things started to go wrong for Dave the fans turned on him. He would often be subjected to abuse in the streets, or on leaving the ground, and so would his wife. David could not handle this. I remember a youth game when somebody was having a go at Dave as he sat on the bench. His critic turned out to be sitting next to Dave's wife, and she really tore into him, quite rightly so because the man was being very abusive. When Dave finally resigned he was relieved: he told me it was like a big weight off his shoulders. He stayed at Norwich and became a coach at the training ground for the Academy, and was very successful there. He has since retired, but still attends the home games. I have a lot of time for Dave Stringer, one of the best.

Ken Brown: 'sensitive to criticism'

Mike Walker: 'still popular with fans'

Martin O'Neill: 'felt cheated'

Mike Walker was the next person in the Carrow Road hotseat. During his playing days Mike was a good goalkeeper, like his son Ian who was later to play for Tottenham, Leicester and England. Mike was making the rare transformation from goalkeeper to football manager. He was also a great talker, a man I could listen to all day. Once you got him started, it was hard to stop him. A brief word with Mike could last for an hour, but he was lovely with it. I got to know him and his wife, Jackie, and his daughter very well indeed. Sadly Jackie died, and that was a great blow to Mike. Adored by Mike and the family, she was at all the home games until she became terminally ill.

On the management side Mike did well. Norwich City finished runners up in the country's top league, and they beat Bayern Munich and got to the semi-final of the European Cup. It was a fantastic achievement. But then Mike wanted to bring in two or three extra players and Robert Chase would not provide the money. So it was inevitable that when Everton approached him with a good offer, he went. The fans were sore, but I do not think they knew the whole story, and Mike felt that Everton was a bigger club and that he was bettering himself.

Mike was not a success at Everton, and the Norwich fans got their revenge when we beat them, and the Barclay End was able to chant, "Walker, Walker, what's the score?"

When Mike left for Everton, his previous number two, John Deehan, took over. John also had played for Norwich and had been a fans' favourite helping the team win the Milk Cup in 1985. In my view he was more a coach than a manager. He was a lovely guy who wanted the team to play attractive football. Players liked him, and so did the crowd until things went wrong and he was asked to leave.

Then came Martin O'Neill, yet another former Norwich player. City had played against Wycombe Wanderers in the FA Cup, when Martin was manager there. We won, but they did quite well, and chairman Robert Chase, a great opportunist, signed him up. Martin was a delightful character. I had much time for him; it was always a pleasure to go to his press conferences on a Thursday, because he would talk about everything, not just football. The O. J. Simpson trial was going on at the time, and we would debate whether he was guilty or not. Martin had a fascination for murder. When he went with Norwich to away matches he would pick up a cab and ask the driver to take him to crime scenes. He was an excellent football manager too, a man with charisma.

He had been promised money to spend, but it did not materialize. As a man who honours his word, Martin expects others to do the same. When somebody breaks that code, for him that is the beginning of the end. He wanted to bring in Dean Windass, and every Thursday we would joke, "Is Dean here?" and his response was always, "No, he's not."

This, of course, was the Chase era. Robert Chase was a very controversial chairman. Much has been said and written about him, but I think on the whole he did a superb job at Norwich City. He lost his way in the last six months, but we should not forget that when Robert took up the reins he saved the club from bankruptcy. He developed it, helped fund the purchase of some key players, and had the foresight to buy that extra land adjoining the ground that is set to make the club a great deal of money.

Arguably he concentrated on financial assets at the expense of players. I always say, "It's lovely having a chocolate box, but if there are no chocolates in it then it is not worth anything." Robert tended to look at things that way. Chase said of Norfolk-born Chris Sutton, whom we sold to Chelsea and who is now with Glasgow Celtic, "If he isn't here at the start of the season then neither will I be," but Chris Sutton was sold and Robert stayed on. The sale of Sutton to Chelsea paid for the new Colney training ground, but Robert's focus on assets rather than players is what really angered the fans.

Occasionally he was opportunistic, as when he brought in Martin O'Neill. But when Martin was denied the funds he thought he had been promised he felt betrayed. Once again the fans were in uproar, and fingers pointed at Robert Chase. Given Martin's success at Glasgow Celtic we can only speculate on whether Norwich might have avoided the long years in the First Division trying to get back to the Premiership.

Chase also upset the fans when City were relegated. He came out with the phrase that Norwich had "no divine right to stay in the Premiership". That made people very angry; in fact the vitriol that was in the press and elsewhere was enormous. Though he spoke his mind, Robert did have his heart in the job. He worked seven days a week at the football club. In a typical day he would travel up to London by train in the morning, come back by lunchtime, do some work and return again to London by car to attend a dinner, and then drive back late at night, all for the club. You have to say he was dedicated. I remember he asked me to come down to his office one Sunday morning and I told him I did not work on Sundays. He worked seven days a week, and he expected others to do the same. He had two secretaries, one for the morning and one for the afternoon. Though he expectd them to work hard I think his staff were treated very well.

Chase's commitment to Norwich City was total. He would very rarely have time off. I remember him flying back in a chartered plane from Blackpool where he was attending an FA conference. He drove over to my house, picked me up, and went on to open a fete in his village. When we arrived at his home his wife greeted us at the door and said, "Happy Birthday Robert." With the fete declared open he drove me back to Norwich, and then flew back to Blackpool. That was the sort of man he was.

But losing Martin O'Neill was a mistake, and I was shocked when I was told by a BBC Radio 5 journalist that he had gone. We were at Filbert Street for a game against Leicester City when my BBC colleague said Martin had not arrived with the team. I immediately sought out Chase, who was having lunch, and he said, "Martin O'Neill is

Gary 'loud-mouth' Megson:
'always shouting at players'

still the Norwich City manager; he is under contract." The board of the day was unable to change his mind. Yet I know Martin would have liked to have remained at Carrow Road. He wanted to put a group together to buy the club, and rang me at the BBC to ask, "How much would it take?"

It didn't take long for Chase to find a replacement; in fact it seems he had the person in mind even as he denied Martin was leaving.

I found his successor, Gary Megson, less approachable and less likeable than O'Neill. Megson was expected to produce a winning team on very limited funds, and that is difficult to do. He was a hard man who expected a lot from his players. When we went to press conferences at Colney he would have us sit in the dressing room with the players while they had a cup of tea, but until the last of them had left would say nothing. You never really questioned Gary Megson. He was quite contentious. I remember one Monday afternoon at Carrow Road when he summoned me into his office and showed me a video of a goal scored the previous Saturday.

"Who scored that goal?" he asked.

I gave him the name of the goal scorer, and he said: "Look at the video."

I said, "Yes, he did score it." He then said "Yes, I know, but why didn't you give it to that other player, because he needs the confidence?" I said, "It's too late, it's been in the papers." This was not the answer he required, nor was it the only time he became abrasive. He would sit me across his desk and tell me: "I don't like what you have been saying on the radio." I told him: "I am sorry, Gary, but until the BBC tells me it doesn't like what I am saying, I'm not going to change." He said, menacingly, "Well that's it - you're on my list." He kept a blacklist of anyone who fell foul of him. He would make a note of their names and would get back at them when he could.

From then on we treated each other with contempt or at a distance. I had to deal with him as a manager, but he gave me short shrift. I was once interviewing a player after a game when Gary came past. A few moments later a club official came up and ordered us to move on. I told him I was in the middle of a BBC interview, and the player reaffirmed this, asking the official to leave us alone. But the official wouldn't have it, and said he had been told to put a stop to it. I am sure Gary was behind it.

Now Gary is at West Bromwich, runners-up to Norwich for the First Division championship, but I still don't get too much out of him. He's a vocal type, always standing at the side of the pitch shouting orders at his players from start to finish. He is hoarse after every game.

Mike Walker came back for a second bite at the cherry, but working this time for a new board and new joint majority shareholders, Michael Wynn-Jones and his wife Delia Smith, both long-standing fans. Returning to a place where you have once been a great success does not always work, and so it proved. But Mike Walker remains very popular at Carrow Road, and from time to time the fans still shout his name.

Mike was replaced by what was described as the "dream team". Bruce Rioch, formerly of Bolton and Arsenal, the man who brought Denis Bergkamp to Highbury, was manager, and Bryan Hamilton was appointed director of football. It was said that what they didn't know about football was not worth knowing, and both had a wealth of experience.

Bruce had been a successful manager at his previous clubs, but at Norwich he was effectively the coach under Hamilton. This arrangement worked for a while, but then results went against them, and there were tensions. Bruce resigned, leaving Hamilton in sole charge. In fact Hamilton secured both jobs on a full-time basis after a win over the old enemy, Ipswich Town. That was about the only memorable moment under his leadership. Norwich plummeted further down the league table, and relegation beckoned.

Bruce Rioch was very good at appraising players, though he did make mistakes. He said to me once that he didn't think Danny Mills would make it, but, as we know, the boy from Sprowston went on to play for England. Bruce himself was a Scottish international. His father was in the armed forces, and was very regimental. Bruce took after him. He demanded a great deal from players, and knew precisely what he wanted from them. It is sad that he has not got another full-time job in football. The longer you are out of the game the fewer people remember you. That is why he tries to keep in touch, still undertakes fitness assignments for the FA, and has kept his home in Broadland.

Bruce is a very entertaining man. We both like country music, and when he was Norwich manager he used to listen to my programme on a Saturday morning. We often discussed country music, and we travelled to Fanfare in America together. In the evenings we would talk football. He would tell some wonderful stories, and I just sat and soaked it up. Sometimes he told me things in confidence about Norwich City Football Club, but I have never reported them, of course. You can't be friends with a manager and then betray him the next day.

I was very sad when he resigned. Like Martin, he said it was because he lacked resources. In his resignation statement he said the club "lacked ambition". He still remains part of Norfolk life, appearing regularly on my country music programme, and we still talk football. He is also a regular at Carrow Road for home games. Despite his parting, he is always welcome in the boardroom, and has a seat in the directors' box, and will have a cup of tea and a chat with the directors at half time.

Norwich is a friendly club. There is no malice towards former employees or even chairmen. Geoffrey Watling is a life president. Robert Chase was invited to a recent reunion of ex-players, but declined.

Robert Chase: 'total commitment'

When Bryan Hamilton departed, he left behind his best signing – an international footballer who had never played in a Norwich shirt. That man, of course, was his assistant, Nigel Worthington. He was not the first candidate for the job; the board was expected to bring someone in from outside, and people like David Jones, now at Wolves, Steve Bruce, now at Birmingham, and many others were bandied about as candidates. But Nigel, supported by Doug Livermore and Steve Foley, fought tenaciously to convince the board he was up to it. Nigel made a strong presentation, arguing the case first to get the club to the top half of the table and then into the Premiership.

He did not pull his punches. He would live within a budget, but it needed to be a better budget. Impressed by his determination, the board appointed him. At the time the fans were less than enthusiastic about the appointment. They wanted a high profile figure. There was also a feeling that Nigel, as Bryan's number two, must have been at least partly responsible for their team's poor league position. But the rest is history and the decision to promote Nigel as manager

after a long line of men passing through the revolving door has turned out to be the most inspired appointment in the club's history.

Nigel is straight as a die, a very honest man. What you see is what you get, no airs and graces. He knows what he wants, and he will tell you about it in no uncertain terms. But he is a very nice person, and is always very happy to talk. We have had a couple of disagreements, but I'm entitled to my opinion, and he's entitled to his. He came on to my afternoon programme, and we talked for an hour about his life. He is a very ambitious manager. He is young, he's learning his trade, and does make mistakes. But he will put up his hands and say, "Yes I was wrong."

I think Nigel has done an exceptional job on limited resources at Carrow Road. He has produced a remarkable side just through wheeling and dealing.

Delia Smith and Michael Wynn-Jones are, of course, crucial to the club's success. Delia has a wonderful passion for Norwich City. She adores it. Long ago, I asked her if she would like to become a director of Norwich. She gave an enigmatic smile and said, "Huh, who knows?" And so it turned

Recipe for success: Delia and Michael welcome Hucks

Nigel Worthington: 'what you see is what you get'

out. Few people would have invested as much as Delia and Michael have in a business for little or no return. Who else would wear a yellow and green scarf everywhere she went?

Delia's toasts are always for the "best football club in the world" and that's Norwich. Her passion has rubbed off on the supporters; they are truly behind her. She has stirred them up.

Financially, the board of directors works very well. In the beginning they were very careful. There were loans that had to be repaid, and unwanted players on three-year contracts to pay off. The fans rallied behind the board because they knew it was trying to rebuild the club to make it financially sound. In future years we will look back and say that Delia and Michael have made a great difference to Norwich City, along with the other directors who work just as hard.

Both Delia and Michael go to every match, home and away, and attend as many functions as possible. Delia will always come on the radio with a message for supporters if asked. As I

lunch in the Gunn Club before every home game, Delia and Michael sit just behind me, so I see a lot of them.

In the Premiership the club will continue to live within its means. It has a very good financial man in Neil Doncaster, who knows how to manage the money. They pay better wages now, but won't give four-year contracts, or pay huge sums to bring players in. Life is going to be tough in 2005 and beyond, so the caution is well-placed.

What I like about Delia and Michael is they are up front. The open evenings are very popular with supporters, and they do not dodge the questions. Nor are they afraid to go into the crowd; in fact Delia often prefers to join the Norwich fans on the terraces at away games.

Chapter 8
The Big Splash

In all my travels over the years with Norwich City nothing sticks more vividly in my mind than two matches against Sunderland in the spring of 2004.

The first was down at Selhurst Park, when they were playing Crystal Palace. Palace had to win to keep their play-off hopes alive. Sunderland had to win to nudge Norwich out of the automatic promotion spot. Better than that, if Sunderland were to lose, or even draw, Norwich would be in the Premiership. Norwich could be promoted without kicking a ball, even if they lost all their remaining games.

I had never undertaken a BBC commentary on a game which did not feature Norwich City, but I persuaded my bosses they should dip their hands in their pockets and spend a few quid on petrol to send Neil and I south to London. It did not take much persuasion. Sky was not planning to cover this crucial match, and Norwich City took my commentary live into Carrow Road, where there was a reserve game playing. Thousands of supporters turned up with their radio sets in the hope that if things went right for us at Selhurst Park there would be the chance to join in a massive celebration that night.

The atmosphere was extraordinary as we approached the kick-off. I was the stranger in the camp. All around me were radio and sports reporters from the national papers, who asked Neil and me lots of questions about Norwich. I had the sense that the success of the Norwich season, especially since Christmas, had rather passed them by. Through my earpiece I was linked up to Carrow Road, and when I reported Crystal Palace's first goal I could hear the roar of the Norwich crowd. Once Palace went two goals ahead you knew that Sunderland weren't going to come back, and when the final whistle went at the reserve match in Norwich the fans continued singing and singing. Like me, they were willing the Palace game to come to an end. When it did, Palace's tails were up, and Ian Dowie's men knew they might be the favourites for the Millennium Stadium. As for Sunderland they had to play us and win to have any hope of a place in the play-offs.

Neil and I jumped into the car and headed for the M11 and Norwich. I called Nigel Worthington on the phone, and could feel the excitement in his voice. "We did it, Roy," he said, taking care not to remind me of my bet with Darren Huckerby. As we got closer to

Norfolk and picked up the signal of Radio Norfolk we realised that there was quite a party going on. We were in high spirits ourselves, and were impatient to get there as we listened to my colleagues describing the scenes at Carrow Road and in the city. When we arrived car horns were blaring, and the pubs were full to overflowing.

Then came the second Sunderland game, up in the North-East on the night of Tuesday May 4. Celebrating promotion, the Norwich management decided the players should make the short one-hour flight up there, rather than the tedious – six or seven – hour drive. Neil and I fell victims to BBC tight budgeting, but were allowed an overnight stay rather than having to drive home after the game. The Canaries played well enough in front of a capacity crowd at the magnificent Stadium of Light, but in the end lost by a single goal. It did not matter. I have never seen a team celebrate a lost game as much as did the Norwich lads. The defeat was academic because our rivals West Bromwich also lost, ending their championship hopes.

Sunderland is almost as far as you can go for an away game. Even so, thousands of fans made the long road journey, while those who could afford it joined a chartered flight from Norwich Airport.

As the news filtered through that Gary Megson's West Bromwich were crumbling, excitement from Canary fans mounted, and the noise from their corner of the stadium became all pervasive. When the game ended our players shook hands with the Sunderland team, who sportingly applauded both the Norwich squad and the Canary supporters.

The good feeling between Sunderland and Norwich stretches back to the "friendly final" in the old Milk Cup, and is lovely to see. What a great game soccer is when tens of thousands of home supporters can provide end of season applause for their rivals, especially given their own disappointment at not making it back to the top flight.

At the end of the Sunderland game I went down to the dressing room area for my usual interviews. I interviewed Delia and Michael, and shared in their joy that their hard work had come to fruition. A steward showed me the way to the changing rooms so I could get the reaction of two or three of the players.

As I approached I could hear an incredible amount of noise coming from the Norwich dressing room. To say the players were in high spirits is an understatement. They were obviously enjoying themselves.

At this point Craig Fleming came out, his face exuding happiness at the outcome of this, his best of seasons. "Craig, can I have a quick word?" I asked.

"Of course you can," he replied, and I pressed the "record" button on my tape machine. During the interview I glanced to my right and saw Robert Green beside me, so I turned to him and asked about a particularly brilliant save he had made. In the middle of the Green interview, out of the corner of my eye I saw Paul Crichton slip out of the dressing room, and wander round behind me. I was suspicious, especially when I realised that Craig was still standing on my left; he had not gone back to join his colleagues for their celebrations.

In the split second before I could react to my suspicion that some trickery was underway, they grabbed me, lifted me up, and dragged me to the dressing room. They took away my tape recorder and microphone and pushed me towards the large post-match tub, where all the players sloshed me with buckets of cold water which had been standing prepared. They also gave me a good walloping with ice-cold wet towels. One of them hit my spectacles before I could get them off, and twisted them.

I was drenched to the skin, and in

my best suit! I could not believe what was happening to me. My first thought was for my equipment and the interviews I had just conducted. Water and tape recorders do not go well together. Meanwhile Craig Fleming and the fitness guy, Dave, had taken over my microphone and were yelling, "We've got Roy Waller! We've got Roy Waller!" This loud and unusual sound bite was going out live on BBC Radio Norfolk.

I was soaked, and freezing, as it was a cold night. From the expression on the players' faces, I could see they found it a highly amusing spectacle. At the time I definitely did not.

Eventually I managed to grab back my microphone and tape recorder, and, to cheers and laughter, escaped from the dressing room. I walked down the tunnel not feeling very happy, and was met by Nigel Worthington, who was equally soaked and bedraggled.

He looked me up and down and said, "Did they get you as well? Ah well, that's a compliment." Feeling a little better, but still shivering with cold, I continued up to the press box to meet incredulous stares. The pressmen filing their stories could not believe the state I was in. Neil Adams cautioned me far too late. "Roy, you should remember you never go near a winning dressing room."

Why didn't you tell me that before I went down there?" I asked him. The answer was a typical Adams grin.
I went back to the dressing room in search of a towel, and ran into several of the players. Thinking they would take pity on me, I asked, plaintively, "Could I have a towel please?"

One replied, "Yes, just pop inside the dressing room, and help yourself."

I snorted: "No way am I going in there again."

Fortunately the kit man from Sunderland was nearby and saw my plight. He took me into their kit room, and gave me a large warm red towel to dry myself off. I have never been so pleased to see a towel in my life.

I went back to my Sunderland hotel still bedraggled and drenched. As I walked in to the foyer to pick up my room key the receptionist asked, "Is it raining outside, pet?"

Chapter 9
A Country Boy

Along with football and Norfolk, the third of the three loves of my professional life is country music. I have been a fan since I was 17, when I was bought a compilation record in vinyl for Christmas. My initial thought was, "Oh, dear," but when I listened to it I thought it was not at all bad. So I used some of the money I was given for Christmas to buy more records, and I really enjoyed them.

Fast-forward 30 years. I had started working part time for BBC Radio Norfolk, and the head of programmes asked me, "Roy, do you know anything about country music?"

"Yes, I do," I replied, and found myself taking over the presentation of a new show from another broadcaster, who was not comfortable in that role. At first the programme ran for half an hour, but I found it difficult to produce the kind of show I wanted in that time and I often overran into the next slot, which did not please the presenter. He complained to the management, and I was ticked off, but then told I could have a full hour.

It is not difficult to fill an hour when you love the subject. I would play my favourite tunes, interview country music people, and run on-air competitions. I realised that to build an audience I would have to do something more. So in my spare time I would go to country music clubs in the county, and invite members to give me dedications for records.

This tactic worked. The audience grew and grew, and it became clear that country music was very popular in Norfolk, particularly in the west of the county. The programme's length was increased to 90 minutes, then to two hours, and then to three hours on a Saturday morning, which was a wonderful slot.

Not everyone likes country music. Neil Adams hates it, for one. But the ratings have been so good that it stays where it is: people from outside Norfolk who can receive our signal listen to it. They write in, mostly requesting the same track, week in week out. This became very monotonous, so it was agreed I would choose to play whatever records I wanted, but my boss insisted we kept the dedications.

He was right. It was not for me to say that listeners should not write a letter, so I always read out all their names without fail.

My regular programmes helped me to become known for something other than football. I was invited to compere a show at the Theatre Royal in Norwich, and since then I have had regular engagements at other theatres, festivals and village halls.

At the same time I came to meet country music stars when they were in Britain. There was Charlie Pride, born to poor sharecroppers in Mississippi and one of seven children, whose golden baritone voice is adored by millions. And Slim Whitman, best remembered for his early-50s hit singles, *Love Song of the Waterfall*, *Indian Love Call*, and *Singing Hills*.

Contrary to many people's beliefs, country music did not begin in the United States, but with fiddlers in Ireland. Nevertheless, I wanted to go to the heart of the present day scene, Nashville, Tennessee. When the opportunity arose for a holiday there, I headed straight for WSM Radio's Grand Ole Opry, famous for live Saturday night broadcasts for almost 80 years. The Opry began with performances by part-time artists who used the show to promote their live appearances throughout the south and middle west. The show has introduced Americans to most, if not all, of the greats of country music. To this day, membership of the Opry remains one of most country music artists' greatest ambitions.

I am not a country music artist, but I wanted to get on to the legendary Opry stage and create my own brand of Nashville sound. At first my request was turned down, but when they heard I was visiting from England they relented and I was told to come back the next day. I did, and went on stage to sing *Little Bitty Tear*. The chorus went like this:

A little bitty tear let me down, spoiled my act as a clown
I had it made up not make a frown, but a little bitty tear let me down.

As I busked my way through the lyrics, I became quite emotional, as I thought of all the stars that had stood on this stage long before this middle-aged man from Norwich.

Since then I have been back to the United States several times. One memorable trip was a holiday with our friend Bruce Rioch, the former Norwich City manager, when we went to Nashville. There we listened to and interviewed country music stars like George Jones and Alan Jackson, to name but two.

It was on one of those trips to America that I had one of my most hair-raising experiences. I was invited to attend the final of the World Cup in Los Angeles, and duly arrived at the stadium to find myself just in front of the actor Dustin Hoffman, the star of *The Graduate*. There were lots of other familiar faces from Hollywood around.

When the game was over there was a bit of a scramble for the exits, and a certain amount of confusion. My wife was swallowed up in the crowd. I suddenly found myself surrounded by a posse of uniformed American policemen. I turned to my left, and came face to face with President George Bush, Senior. Incredulous, I was not too sure what to do. So I met his gaze, clasped his hand, shook it, and said, "Very pleased to meet you." He smiled, and replied cordially, "Very pleased to meet you." Seconds later the police lunged at me, grabbed my arms and unceremoniously shoved me out of the way. One said to me, brusquely: "You know, you could have been shot." I said: "Why? Why?" He said: "You made a grab for the president. You can count yourself a very lucky man." I made my way back to my hotel and called my mother, and she said, "Goodness me, Roy, you might not have been seen again."

Back in Norwich I was to meet another celebrity who has since played a big role in my country music life. The Irish impresario Dick Condon invited me

With Daniel O'Donnell at the stage door: 'a firm friend'

down to the Theatre Royal, saying, "I have a young Irish man coming tonight who I think is going to do well – will you come and have a listen?" I stood at the back of the theatre to get a good perspective, although there were not a lot of people in the audience, and most of them were Irish and seemed to know him. After his performance, I said, "Dick, what is this guy's name? He is fantastic." He took me backstage and introduced me to Daniel O'Donnell. The rest is history.

Daniel O'Donnell's rags to riches success story couldn't have happened to a more popular and talented performer. Coming from a very musical family in Donegal he has become one of Ireland's greatest showbusiness personalities, performing to over 300,000 people every year. He has been in concert at Carnegie Hall, the Sydney Opera House, the Royal Albert Hall, Wembley Arena and many other venues. Some of his international concerts are booked out months in advance.

But he always makes time for BBC Radio Norfolk and me. He has been to our studios many times, and we have recorded one or two hour-long documentaries. I got to know him very well, and he has become a firm friend.

When I took a party of country music listeners across to Ireland, he came over to our hotel and and joined us in some impromptu songs. We have also been on television together, and listeners will know that hardly a week goes by when I do not play one of his numbers.

Strictly speaking, Daniel is not a country singer, but he sings country songs. He appeals particularly to women, who regard him as the "boy next door". When he came on stage in his silver grey suit, the girls would go berserk. A lot of listeners' hearts were broken when he eventually married.

Daniel is special. He can be on stage for two hours or more, and then spend another two hours talking to fans after the performance. He has a wonderful memory for people and faces, sometimes recalling an incident years before. I took my wife and her sister to see Daniel when he was on stage in Ipswich, and he looked at Sylvie's sister and said, "How lovely to see you again;" he had remembered her from three years before.

Fans love him for this. Daniel will telephone people whom he has heard are seriously ill to wish them well. He has made enormous efforts for young Romanian orphans by providing homes and support.

There are other Irish performers, of course, though not in the same league as Daniel, who have this warmth for their fans, a contrast with some bands and artists in England who more often than not finish their shows and then are off. I think that is very sad, because it is the fans who have put them where they are and deserve to be rewarded with time and attention.

I love country music for its simplicity. It's about life. You hear criticism that these are corny old songs about old men with gangrenous legs, and so on. But they are not. Country music is about children, love, marriage, divorce, and death. Those who write and perform it write about their experiences. My friend Raymond Froggatt has written lyrics for Cliff Richard and Daniel O'Donnell, and is himself a performer.

Froggie started his life as a pipe lagger, but spent his evenings singing in pubs, and his spare time secretly writing poetry. Now with his own band, his shows are sold out across Britain. He has huge support from fans who turn up waving green frogs and laughing at his wonderful sense of humour. His patter between songs is second-to-none. I have compered his shows all over East Anglia, and several times at Hunstanton, where he has a tremendous following. If he has three nightly performances the fans will come

three times to hear the man I call the "master".

Raymond has the ability to throw open his curtains in the morning and to write a song about what he sees. Daniel O'Donnell recently commissioned him to write about 15 songs - a tremendous compliment. If the album is successful, Froggie will do very well out of it.

As with Daniel, I first met Raymond at the Theatre Royal. I had gone there to interview Tammy Wynette, another performer with humble beginnings and now the first lady of country music. Tammy was from Nashville and top of the bill. Raymond and his band were there in support. I liked what I heard from this strange man who dangled his legs over the edge of the stage. What magnificent songs, and what a voice! Later we became great friends, and I now act as his compere when he appears in East Anglia. He is a lovely and genuine person to work with. Chatting with him in his dressing room, I would marvel at his ability to listen to the words of his own songs through his headphones while at the same time reading a book. I have never been able to do that.

The big stars this side of the Atlantic do not have the status of their American counterparts, and certainly not the money. Most of them have to pay to produce their own records, but they are good performers, to be sure.

Producing my country music show is very different from the other work I do, and is really a labour of love. It takes up a small part of every working day, and then I go into the studios at the Forum early on Saturday mornings to present it. During the football season, when I am away with Norwich City, I record it on a Friday afternoon.

But the work begins on Monday when the first batch of letters arrives. There are also emails and text messages containing dedications, and I read them all before I start scripting. Each day I add a little more, trying

Roy with his friend Froggie

always to get everyone in. Then the records that I am to play have to be selected. Sylvie often helps with this, as she has a good ear for what people like. She selects some tracks and plays them to me. The programme has changed over the years. I no longer review albums, or run a competition. If there are country music stars or writers visiting the area, I will invite them into the studio to pick their favourite six numbers, which freshens up the programme. I used to allocate an hour to one particular artist, but an hour is a long time for a listener to put up with someone he or she may not like, so I have reduced that to half an hour.

Of course you are never going to please everybody, but if I please 80 per cent of my listeners then I will have done a good job. There are always moaners who say I play too much Irish, or too much American, and others who complain that I talk too much. I tell listeners about country music events in Norfolk, and the coming weekend's performances, and those of the following week and weekend. Country music is alive and well in Norfolk! I see it as a service to the fans, to the artists and event organizers.

It is important to remember that many of those who provide this wonderful entertainment do so on a shoestring budget for very little reward - and sometimes none at all - only a moaning Granddad who complains that he didn't like their songs. Sometimes my BBC bosses ask me why I plug events that are across the Norfolk border, but my show is listened to wherever the signal reaches, and that extends into Cambridgeshire and Suffolk, and even parts of Lincolnshire and Essex. You can't stop people listening if they wish to! When out in their cars, they do not stop listening because there is a county border. BBC Radio Suffolk now also has a country music programme, and we coordinate our times so that we do not clash. I am sure that many people in south Norfolk

The Princess at Hunstanton:
Roy's favourite town

listen to the Suffolk programme, as those south of the border listen to ours.

Many country music followers are not drawn by loyalty to a particular club. They tend to go to the venue where they know the artist they like is performing. They pick and choose. The result is that many clubs fall by the wayside, because if you pay a band three hundred pounds and you take only two hundred at the door or on the bar you are in trouble. It has been suggested to me that I should run a club or a country music festival, but I prefer to remain a compere. I love my compere spot at the Princess Theatre in my favourite Norfolk town of Hunstanton. There is something about that place that makes it extra special; perhaps it's the buildings, maybe it's the coastline or the atmosphere created by the people who both live and visit there.

Both at shows and on the BBC, I have to take care to be even-handed in my choice of music. At the BBC I am under strict instructions not to put to air anything that does not sound right. Playing a poor quality recording would be a disservice to the artist. On one occasion I was sent a recorded tape that had a budgerigar in the background! Actually the budgie sounded better than the artist. My advice to anyone seeking a career in country music, full – or part-time, is to go to a professional studio to record. You have to speculate to accumulate.

Chapter 10

My County, My Life

For as long as I can, I want more of the same. More live radio, more success for Norwich City, more country music, and the dream of commentaries from Europe. But I will not leave Norfolk. When I was with the Automobile Association I could have moved to London or the Midlands, but I always turned the offers down. I would have none of it.

I worry about the future. I just hope they don't end up spoiling this county of mine. I particularly do not want Norfolk to end up looking like any other county. People have escaped from other counties to come and live here, so Norfolk is in danger of becoming just like the rest. There are plans for more housing, faster roads, and for a regional form of government, which looks as if it will be based in Cambridge. I am not sure of the benefits of any of this.

Many of the people who, like me, were born and bred in Norfolk would like it to stay as it is, or even like it was. It is a super county. You can get to the seaside in half an hour from almost anywhere, there is little crime, though it has been increasing and that is a cause for concern. Norfolk is littered with people who used to come here on holiday, but now have chosen to live here. Many former Norwich City footballers have come back to live. Newcomers will tell you they are very reluctant to leave, so we must be doing something right; we must be offering something that other counties cannot provide.

It is a widely held belief that Norfolk people do not like strangers and sometimes resent their presence. That is not the case. We are wary of newcomers, but when we get to know them we accept them. But some people come here from other parts of Britain and try to change my county. I get very upset when they say it is essential that we build a new by-pass. Why should we? If they do not like life without a by-pass why did they come here?

I remember having a debate on the radio with a woman who had just moved to Norwich from London. She said: "It's all very nice, but I think the roads are terrible."

"Didn't you know that when you moved up here?" I asked.

"Oh yes," she said, "but if we had better roads we could open up everything."

We do not want that. We are very happy that the pace of life is different in

Norwich's historic Guildhall, near the BBC's Forum headquarters

Norfolk. High flyers from London come down here because of the quality of life, and the absence of hustle and bustle. In London nobody knows you; you are an island. Here people will stop and say "good morning" or "good afternoon".

This is not to say we should not have some change, but we need to be careful. We should not change things just for the sake of it. Much has changed since I was a boy in Mile Cross, and not always for the better. The old Hippodrome was knocked down, and I think that was a mistake. Other buildings have been demolished though they were worth preserving. Some very ugly buildings have gone up, like Norfolk Tower, where the BBC used be.

The industrial landscape is also very different from when I was a boy. In the shoe manufacturing industry, Norwich was second only to Northampton, and whole families would work at Bally or other companies producing footwear for high street shops like Dolcis and Lilley and Skinner. Mother, father, son and daughter might all cycle together to the same factory. It was a good life for them, but sadly it all came to an end.

Then there were the great chocolate factories. I used to cycle round Chapelfield, and get the exciting sweet whiff of molten chocolate at the Macintosh factory. Then, that company merged with Rowntree in York, and the Norwich production plant was shut down. Then Rowntree Macintosh was taken over by the Swiss, and that was the end of it. At least we still have Caleys left to nurture my childhood memories.

Most of the industries were family concerns owned by Norfolk people. Laurence and Scott was a famous electrical engineering giant down in Thorpe. There was Colmans' mustard factory near Carrow Road, owned by the Colman family who were also active in the county's politics and in the *Eastern Daily Press* and *Eastern Evening News*. But the mustard

Pull's Ferry: definitely a 'Fine City'

business has now been bought by the multinational company Unilever, which also owns Bird's Eye, Walls and many of the soap brands we buy. The Norwich Union once boasted that it had a job for every school leaver in Norfolk with a General Certificate of Education. That is sadly no longer true and, like some of the manufacturers before it, NU has been swallowed up in a bigger company that now prefers to be known as Aviva. Times have changed and you can no longer be safe in a job in Norfolk.

What we have now are service industries and lots of call centres, but as time goes by even some of those jobs are moving away to South India.

We have also lost some of Norfolk's great characters. There were seafarers, fishermen and lifeboat men like the great Henry 'Downtide' West. There were farmers and characters from the land. People who retained the great Norfolk dialect. We shall in time look back and regret very much that we did

not record their memories as oral history for future generations to enjoy. People are now asking, "Why did we not get all this down on tape?"

On my programmes when I suggest we talk about things that happened years ago, the lights start flashing and people call from around the county with stories they want to share with the audience. It seems everyone has a tale of the Norfolk of years ago. It is the same in the press. Derek James of the *Eastern Evening News* writes a column about memories of Norfolk's past, and is constantly amazed at the number of people who write or call with interesting material. Norfolk and Norwich are full of history and characters, like Edith Cavell, Elizabeth Fry and many others.

Many of our sporting arenas have gone, like Norwich Speedway. After an afternoon at Carrow Road there was nothing better than a trip to The Firs at Hellesdon and an evening of speedway with some of the best riders in the country. But then greed came into the

In Norfolk you are never far from the sea

picture, and The Firs was sold as a housing estate. Speedway still flourishes at King's Lynn, but despite many an attempt, the sport has not been brought back to Norwich. When I open up the phone lines and mention speedway the phones ring and ring.

For the future, we have to protect Norfolk from the kind of urban sprawl you find in Essex, but we must also improve Norfolk's transport connections. There is always a big argument about roads in Norfolk. Some believe that it is better to keep the roads as they are because it will dissuade too many people from coming here, but I am not so sure.

Better access roads are essential. There is no doubt that it is difficult to get in and out of the county, particularly in summer time when traffic jams build up through Thetford Forest, and can add an hour to the journey. Better links would undoubtedly help commerce, and

encourage more businesses to invest here.

I would hate to be a planner, working away in County Hall or at the offices of one of our district councils. These days they have so many applications and inquiries, and are under pressure from developers on the one side and conservationists on the other. It must be very difficult to strike a balance. Those who have lived in our county for a long time will say, "It's all gone wrong, it's not like it used to be." Well, I think we do remember the good things in life, but do not always recall the bad. It's just like the weather: people remember the long hot summers, but not the really dreadful ones. But there is truth in the argument that in recent years it has not all been progress. As a boy I would walk out of my house at eight o'clock in the morning, and return again at seven at night. Nobody worried. I would knock on people's doors and ask for a glass of water. You cannot do that any more. Apart from the risks, it is not socially acceptable, but to me such boyhood days were a great adventure. As children we would wander out, and explore. There were seasons – the conker season, the marbles season, and the popgun season. In the summer we swam in the river Wensum, and in the winter we would walk across to the shallow frozen dykes, and enjoy skating. We would make a popgun out of elderberry and fire acorns. The children of today miss all that. Instead they are stuck indoors watching television or playing computer games, some of them fairly mindless.

This, of course, is nostalgia. We have to address the present, and I think it is important to preserve the unique character of Norfolk. It should not be concreted over and become an urban sprawl. We do not want to be like Essex. We want Norfolk to stay like Norfolk.

Our magnificent cathedral provides inspiration and focus

Chapter 11
Radio Active

When I was a boy, what we now call radio was known as the wireless. To me it was a magical box in bakelite standing in the corner of the living room through which you could hear voices from all over the world and visualise what was happening. There was fun, entertainment and, of course, music. There were programmes like *The Goons* and *Dick Barton, Special Agent*. Entertainment seemed to be the main aspect of radio, though there were news bulletins at certain times during the day, and weather forecasts. At the time there was only the BBC. Commercial radio stations like Broadland did not arrive until much later so if you wanted to listen to music you had what was called then the BBC Light Programme. The other channels were the BBC Home Service, a little like BBC Radio 4 but much more solemn, and the Third Programme, which played classical music and Shakespeare. There was no local radio: that did not really start until I began my football commentaries from Carrow Road.

Some people used to say that television would mean the death of radio: I remember they also said newspapers would die. Nothing of the kind has happened, and radio has had a considerable resurgence, particularly with channels like Radio Five Live and local radio.

New technology has worked in favour of radio. Our recording equipment is lighter and easier to operate. Digital sound provides superb quality, and the new digital radios now on sale provide flawless reception. The introduction of digital communications, which transmit most of our long distance phone calls, means that there is none of that crackle and interference we used to get, for instance, when my away football commentaries were sent to Norwich on an ordinary BT phone line. Being digital means that we can call up anyone anywhere in the world and put him or her on air in seconds. On a more prosaic level most people in Norfolk commute to work by car, and on any journey into the congested roads of Norwich our traffic reports are essential listening.

Thanks to the internet our reach is much greater too. The limited frequencies we have mean that our normal wireless signal can only be heard by people in Norfolk and some of the adjoining counties. But there are people who live outside Norfolk, indeed

Norwich Castle: link with the past

outside the country, who still want to keep in touch with what goes on here, be it Norwich City Football Club, the races at Fakenham or my country music programme.

All they have to do is to turn on their computers, connect to the Internet, go to *www.bbc.co.uk/norfolk* and they will find they can listen to one or two of our programmes. My football commentaries are broadcast on the Norwich City website, Canaries World, and I have heard from people in Sydney, Australia who get up at two in the morning to listen to them. The time may not be far away when all the programming is on the Internet: it is technically feasible, though when you play records there is always the problem of rights and things like that.

Radio is such a great medium for interactivity. If I want to know the answer to a question, I have only to pose it on air and within minutes several people will have telephoned in with the answer. There is always someone out there who will relate to the problem, and come on and tell me. This does not happen in any other media to the same extent, not even the Internet.

To me it is a pity that local radio is the poor relation of broadcasting, and I told the top BBC executives this when I went to a course in Bristol not long ago. They took exception to my view, and said that local radio plays a very important part in broadcasting, more so than ever, and that the BBC is putting more money into it. I hope that proves to be the case, for on local radio you are talking to the people in your county, relating to their problems, and the issues they care about.

A typical example of this was when a story appeared in the newspapers that Norwich City Council planned to dismantle the signs that say, "Welcome to Norwich, a Fine City." There was an immediate reaction against the plan. People thought it was a terrible decision. So I got the chairman on air and he promptly denied it, and said the story was untrue. Whether it was or not, the fact is that the publicity knocked the idea on the head. That is local radio at work in the interests of the community.

Postscript

As I look back over the years I realise how lucky I have been. I have achieved so much that perhaps the ordinary man in the street would never have the opportunity to do. But as the saying goes: Whoever you are, you only get out of life what you put into it.

I have made mistakes, but then don't we all? Hopefully I have learnt from them.

There are so many things left that I would like to achieve. When I talk to young people I make the point that if they are offered a new opportunity, they should accept it and then get on with it. The fear vanishess once you have done it and you move on.

I worried about my debut on stage, standing in the centre circle of a football pitch with Steve Cram entertaining a crowd of 45,000, running with the Queen's jubilee torch, and being gunged live on the Noel Edmunds Show. But I achieved these feats and would have no fear being in similar circumstances again.

I have mentioned the Robert Chase era and many people have wondered about the true story behind Robert leaving the football club. A short while ago Robert approached me, willing to talk live on the radio about what went on behind the scenes at Carrow Road, and how it all came about. We at the BBC decided that an interview of this kind should be pre-recorded, but Robert declined to do it that way. One day the truth will emerge and I sincerely hope that I will be there when the opportunity arises.

So what of the future? "When is he going to retire?" I can hear people asking. I will know when the right moment comes. Despite missing this fabulous lifestyle, I will hand over my microphone to a member of the younger generation, and sincerely hope that, whoever that is, he or she gets as much satisfaction as I have had over the years.

I have asked that when I die my ashes are to be scattered in the Barclay End goal mouth at Carrow Road. From there, I will be supporting my yellow and green heroes for ever.

Bryan Gunn's Leukaemia Appeal & East Anglian Air Ambulance

By buying this book you have helped two local charities.

Norfolk-based *Grice Chapman Publishing* is very pleased to support Bryan Gunn's Leukaemia Appeal and the East Anglian Air Ambulance. For every book sold we shall give £1 to be shared by the two charities.

Bryan Gunn's Appeal was set up in 1993 after Bryan and Susan lost their daughter Françesca to childhood leukaemia at the age of two. At that time Norwich City were playing at the top of the newly-formed Premier league, and representing Britain in the UEFA Cup, with Bryan playing brilliantly in goal for the Canaries. We were in the Carrow Road crowd to watch the poignant moment when Bryan turned out to play for the club just days after Françesca's tragic death, and we will always remember it.

The public of Norwich and Norfolk have responded generously to Bryan's appeal and by October 2004 had raised over £700,000. In 1994 the Appeal founded the Françesca Gunn Laboratory at the University of East Anglia, and has funded several pioneering research projects there, helping to make UEA one of the foremost cancer research centres in the world today.

You can learn more about Bryan Gunn's Leukaemia Appeal or make a donation at www.gaps.uk.com
and the East Anglian Air Ambulance at www.eastanglianairambulance.org.uk.

Colin Chapman
Simon Chapman
Susan Grice

Directors
Grice Chapman Publishing

© Eastern Daily Press